IMAGES OF ASIA
Series Adviser: SYLVIA FRASER-LU

Borobudur

Titles in the series

At the Chinese Table
T. C. LAI

Balinese Paintings (2nd ed.)
A. A. M. DJELANTIK

Bamboo and Rattan:
Traditional Uses and Beliefs
JACQUELINE M. PIPER

The Birds of Java and Bali
DEREK HOLMES and
STEPHEN NASH

The Birds of Sumatra and
Kalimantan
DEREK HOLMES and
STEPHEN NASH

Borobudur (2nd ed.)
JACQUES DUMARÇAY

The Chinese House: Craft,
Symbol, and the Folk Tradition
RONALD G. KNAPP

Chinese Jade
JOAN HARTMAN-GOLDSMITH

Early Maps of South-East Asia
(2nd ed.)
R. T. FELL

Folk Pottery in South-East Asia
DAWN F. ROONEY

Fruits of South-East Asia: Facts
and Folklore
JACQUELINE M. PIPER

A Garden of Eden: Plant Life in
South-East Asia
WENDY VEEVERS-CARTER

The House in South-East Asia
JACQUES DUMARÇAY

Images of the Buddha in Thailand
DOROTHY H. FICKLE

Indonesian Batik: Processes,
Patterns and Places
SYLVIA FRASER-LU

Japanese Cinema: An Introduction
DONALD RICHIE

The Kris: Mystic Weapon of the
Malay World (2nd ed.)
EDWARD FREY

Life in the Javanese Kraton
AART VAN BEEK

Macau
CESAR GUILLEN-NUÑEZ

Mammals of South-East Asia
(2nd ed.)
EARL OF CRANBROOK

Mandarin Squares: Mandarins
and their Insignia
VALERY M. GARRETT

The Ming Tombs
ANN PALUDAN

Musical Instruments of
South-East Asia
ERIC TAYLOR

Old Bangkok
MICHAEL SMITHIES

Old Manila
RAMÓN MA. ZARAGOZA

Old Penang
SARNIA HAYES HOYT

Old Singapore
MAYA JAYAPAL

Sarawak Crafts: Methods,
Materials, and Motifs
HEIDI MUNAN

Silverware of South-East Asia
SYLVIA FRASER-LU

Songbirds in Singapore:
The Growth of a Pastime
LESLEY LAYTON

Traditional Chinese Clothing in
Hong Kong and South China
1840–1980
VALERY M. GARRETT

Borobudur

Second Edition

JACQUES DUMARÇAY

Translated and edited by
MICHAEL SMITHIES

SINGAPORE
OXFORD UNIVERSITY PRESS
OXFORD   NEW YORK
1991

Oxford University Press

Oxford New York Toronto
Delhi Bombay Calcutta Madras Karachi
Petaling Jaya Singapore Hong Kong Tokyo
Nairobi Dar es Salaam Cape Town
Melbourne Auckland
and associated companies in
Berlin Ibadan

Oxford is a trade mark of Oxford University Press

First published as an Oxford University Press paperback 1978
Sixth impression 1989
Second edition in Images of Asia 1991

Published in the United States by
Oxford University Press, Inc., New York

ISBN 0 19 588550 3

British Library Cataloguing in Publication Data

Dumarçay, Jacques
Borobudur. 2nd ed.—(Images of Asia)
I. Title   II. Smithies, Michael, 1932–
III. Series
959.82

ISBN 0-19-588550-3

Library of Congress Cataloging-in-Publication Data

Dumarçay, Jacques.
Borobudur/Jacques Dumarçay; translated and edited by
Michael Smithies.—2nd ed.
p.   cm.—(Images of Asia)
Includes bibliographical references and index.
ISBN 0-19-588550-3:
1. Borobudur (Temple: Magelang, Indonesia)   2. Temples—
Indonesia—Magelang—Conservation and restoration.
I. Smithies, Michael, 1932–   II. Title.   III. Series.
NA6026.6.B6D8513   1992
726'.143'095982—dc20
91-28860
CIP

Printed in Malaysia by Peter Chong Printers Sdn. Bhd.
Published by Oxford University Press Pte. Ltd.,
Unit 221, Ubi Avenue 4, Singapore 1440

Preface

BOROBUDUR attracts a huge number of sightseers, both Indonesian and foreign. With the great increase in recent years of tourism to the country, Borobudur, now surrounded by a landscaped park and with the more obvious gimcrack stalls removed from sight, is a prime destination for visitors. But on public holidays, such as the Indonesian National Day on 17 August and Lebaran, at the end of Ramadan, the crush of local visitors is such that a one-way system on the stairways has to be enforced, and it is best to avoid trying to see the monument at such times, as well as on Sundays, when large parties of visitors come.

The monument naturally means different things to different people, and visitors come for a number of reasons, but the late Sultan Hamengku Buwono IX of Yogyakarta, a former Vice-President of the Indonesian Republic, noted that Indonesians considered it was built 'as a place of meditation, not of worship'.

The restoration work on the monument, and particularly its dismantling, gave me the chance to study the internal structure of Borobudur and appreciate its history better. In this text only a general survey is given, taking no account of the numerous changes in, for example, the doorways over so many years.

Overseas visitors who have often heard of Borobudur are sometimes unaware of the equally important temples in the Prambanan area, a few kilometres to the north-east of Yogyakarta: the huge Hindu shrine of Prambanan itself, Sambisari, the Buddhist *candi* of Kalasan, Sari, Sewu, and Plaosan, and the so-called palace of Ratu Boko, to name the most outstanding. These need to be considered in relation to Borobudur, and are described more fully in my book *The Temples of Java*.

This text first appeared in 1978 and has gone through many printings since. I hope this revised edition will satisfy visitors with its explanations.

Paris   JACQUES DUMARÇAY
May 1991

Contents

Preface		*v*
1	The Historical Setting	1
2	The Religious Setting	6
3	The Architectural Setting	13
4	The Architecture of the Monument	21
5	Buddhist Architecture in the Ninth Century	47
6	Rediscovery and Restoration	57
7	Conclusion	65
	Glossary	68
	Select Bibliography	70
	Chronological Table	73
	Index	74

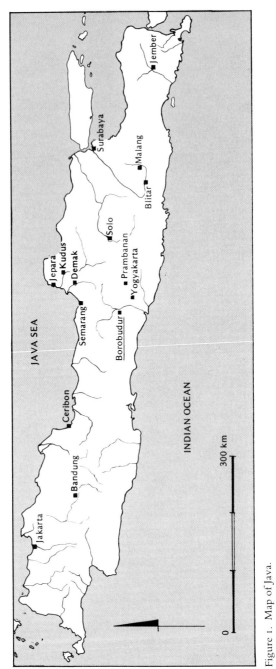

Figure 1. Map of Java.

I

The Historical Setting

THE two main historical sources for the states of the early period in the Indonesian archipelago are the inscriptions left by the rulers and dignitaries of its Hindu kingdoms and Chinese chronicles. These sources give very limited information. The inscriptions mostly describe religious foundations and the Chinese chronicles are principally concerned with embassies sent to the imperial court.

The Hindu Period

The Hindu period in the states in the archipelago, and more generally in southern Asia, was not brought about by force. There was no conquest or colonization as with the European countries in the nineteenth century. The Hindu penetration was brought about by cultural and, especially, religious circumstances, by the use of Sanskrit for inscriptions, and the adoption of a complete and coherent Hindu or Buddhist mythology. This was not the domain of traders. At the time when it is generally agreed that the Hindu period was beginning in the area, in the first centuries of the Christian era, it is likely that Sanskrit in India was already no longer a truly living language but restricted to religious affairs.

The Hindu period was most likely brought about by the influence of priests dependent on small existing kingdoms. These were inextricably associated with the irrigation systems and a religion which allowed for the deification of rulers' origins. The great success of Mahayana Buddhism, as will be seen later, was assured since it permitted the assimilation of the king to a Bodhisattva (a future Buddha) and so reinforced the temporal authority of the ruler. It would seem, therefore, that for a large part Hindu influence was due to the initiative of princes in the archipelago who attracted Brahmins and perhaps artisans to their courts. Although Chinese influence is not as strong as Indian, it is technically discernible in the wooden buildings and also in the use of tiles.

The first Hindu institution in Java of which record has come down to us is mentioned in the Sanskrit inscriptions of about AD 450 from the south of Jakarta. Their author was Purnavarman, a king of Taruma, and one of these inscriptions mentions the opening of a canal.

Sailendra and Sanjaya

In Java, between the inscriptions of Purnavarman in the fifth century and the Cangal inscription of 732 on Gunung Wukir near Borobudur, records are sketchy and uninteresting and their interpretation uncertain. The author of the Cangal text, King Sanjaya, was probably a Mataram prince but about whom little is known. His successor, King Panongkaran, is cited in the Kalasan inscription of 778. He was only a tributary king to the Sailendra dynasty. This may also be the case for Sanjaya. De Casparis, after examining all the information in the Sailendra dynasty inscriptions, concluded that during the period from the end of the eighth century to the beginning of the ninth century, two dynasties shared power in central Java in the following way:

Sanjaya (Hindu)	Sailendra (Buddhist)
Sanjaya 732–±760	Bhanu 752–?
Panongkaran ±760–778–±780	Visnu (Dharmatunga)?– 775–782
Panunggalan ±780–±800	Indra (Sangramadhanomjaya) 782–812–before 824
Warak ±800–before 819 or 829	Samaratunga 824–832
Garung (= Patapan?) 819–829–842	
Pikatan 842–850–856	
Kayuwani 856–863–882	

The dates in italics are confirmed by an inscription; the others were established by de Casparis.

For the dates of Indra and Samaratunga, a correction has been proposed: 784 to 792 for Indra and 792 to about 833 for Samaratunga. After 833, de Casparis thinks that the Sanjaya became completely independent of the Sailendra.

The appearance of the Sailendra in Java is an event of great importance for the origin of Borobudur, since it is this dynasty which established Mahayana Buddhism and caused the Hindu worshippers who had constructed the Dieng temples to move eastward. This eastward movement is confirmed by a Sanskrit inscription dating from 760 discovered in the Malang region and mentioning the construction of a temple dedicated to Agastya. The Chinese chronicles also tell of the displacement of the capital to the east. During this relatively short period from 760 to 800, the Sailendra dynasty probably established suzerainty over Cambodia and tried several times, in 767, 774, and 787, to establish themselves without much success on the east coast of Indo-China. About 800, in the reign of Indra, the power of the dynasty experienced a certain decline and it was at this point, in 802, that the Khmer prince Jayavarman II definitively freed himself of all subservience to Java.

Coedès thought that towards 820 the Hindus who had emigrated to the east regained power by reuniting central and east Java. This would be connected with the Sanjaya dynasty which was completely freed of the suzerainty of the Sailendra in 832–833. This Hindu renaissance showed itself in the construction of the whole ensemble of Prambanan, the consecration date of which is 856. In spite of this return of Hinduism, which must have been accompanied by a new cultural wave from India, Buddhism continued to flourish. The reigning princes founded several new temples and made gifts to Buddhist sanctuaries. In 860 and 873, the Chinese emperor sent embassies to Java. An echo of this visit can be found in the *New History of the Tang* (quoted in Pelliot) which says that the Javanese 'make fortifications of wood, and even the big houses are covered in palm thatch. They have ivory beds and matting made of the bark of bamboo. The country produces tortoise-shell, gold, silver, rhinoceros horns and ivory. . . . They have an alphabet and have a knowledge of astronomy.'

It is difficult, therefore, to decide which ruler undertook the construction of Borobudur, but recent excavations carried out at Candi Sewu have allowed some refinement to the previously known history of architecture in the region. As noted above, at the beginning of the eighth century, the Sanjaya dynasty extended its power over the central part of Java at least as far as Gunung Wukir and its suzerainty was acknowledged on the south coast, since the builder of the first state of Candi Kalasan still recognized its power in 778. The excavations at Candi Sewu have made it clear that the cult of the five Jinas, also celebrated at Borobudur, was only practised in this temple from its second state, after 792.

Numerous scholars have acknowledged the duality of Borobudur: its pyramidal appearance with its numerous horizontal levels, and the hemispherical aspect of its outer casing which is unmistakably Buddhist. The dismantling of the structure allowed the stepped pyramid without its casing to become apparent. It forms a whole and is without reliefs; the master builder, to increase the apparent height of the building, used perspective effects common in this period in Sivaite buildings in Java.

In consequence of these new pieces of information, we believe that Borobudur was laid out by a Hindu Sanjaya king and that in its first state it was conceived as the base of a Sivaite temple. Then, around 790, the powerful Buddhist Sailendra kings pushed the Sanjaya northwards; when the Sailendra reached the upper reaches of the Progo (they also went as far as Dieng), they found Borobudur incomplete. They probably considered it was impossible to leave so significant a symbol of Sivaite power, so they resumed work on the monument and gave it its Buddhist character.

The Sanjaya then re-established themselves and in 832 they brought the centre of Java under their sway, but, unlike the Sailendra, showed themselves more tolerant and only carried out limited works at Borobudur without changing its Buddhist orientation. The chronology is thus:

730 Foundation of Sanjaya power and rule
732 Inscription of Candi Cangal on Gunung Wukir
±750 Construction of the temples at Dieng
±775 Laying out of the first state of Borobudur
±790 Work on the first state of Borobudur stopped
792 Inscription of Candi Sewu
±795 Beginning of the work on the second state of Borobudur
±820 End of work on the third state
832 Reunification of the centre of Java by the Sanjaya and resumption of work on Borobudur
856 Consecration of Prambanan temple
±860 End of work on Borobudur

After this last date, the monument continued to be used until the tenth century; Tang period potteries have been found at the site. Some activity doubtless continued to the fourteenth century at least, and the monument is probably referred to in the *Negarakertagama*, a Javanese text of the mid-fourteenth century. Its author greatly admired the Vajradhara Buddhist sect and lists the main shrines where the sect practised its rites at the time he was writing. One of them is called Budur, which is most probably Borobudur (Canto 77, Stanza 3).

2

The Religious Setting

THERE is little documentary evidence to consult when attempting to determine the religious environment at the time of the building of Borobudur. There are some inscriptions, the statues and reliefs of Borobudur itself and other contemporary monuments, and a few subsequent texts which can be linked to its architectural symbolism, in particular the *Sang Hyang Kamahayanikan*, a Sanskrit catechism which is linked with a text in Old Javanese. Using these sources, it has been concluded that Mahayanist Buddhism prevailed in the creation of Borobudur, alongside a general belief in the five Jinas (the Dhyani Buddhas), and a special cult attached to the Bodhisattvas and to the Goddess Tara.

Buddhism is a doctrine of salvation which in some essential elements stems from Hinduism. The doctrine was preached for the first time by the Buddha whose name was Siddartha Gautama and who belonged to the Sakya clan, whence the name Sakyamuni (the sage of the Sakya clan) by which he was often known. He was born about 563 BC at Lumbini, near Kapilavastu, at the foot of the Himalayas in a small state ruled by his father. When Siddartha was sixteen years old, he married and had a son. The soothsayers at the time of his birth had indicated that he would not become king if he saw an old, sick, or dead person and every effort was made to prevent him seeing them. However, about 537 BC revelation came to him through encounters with age, sickness, and death. He was revolted by the world, left his family, and became a wandering mystic. He first of all practised yoga but doubted the validity of the method for, having achieved what should have been a state of ecstasy, he found himself the same as before. He then gave himself over to asceticism, but seeing that he achieved nothing by it he gave up and went to Bodh Gaya. There, under a tree, he sat down to meditate, directing his thoughts to the mystery of death and rebirth. During the night he became enlightened. He continued his meditation for some time and then went to Benares where he preached a sermon which contained the essence of the Buddhist doctrine.

See, brothers, the holy truth about pain; birth is pain, age is pain, sickness is pain, death is pain; union with those one does not like is pain, separation from those one loves is pain, not to succeed in one's aim is pain; the five forms of attachment are pain. See, brothers, the holy truth about the origin of pain; it is desire which leads from one reincarnation to another, accompanied by pleasure and envy, which now and again is satisfied; the desire for pleasure, the desire for the material, and desire for the impermanent. See, brothers, the holy truth of the suppression of pain; the extinction of this desire by the complete destruction of desire. Desire is banished and forsaken; one is liberated from it and it has no further place. (After Foucher.)

The cycle of rebirths (*samsara*) has its origin in eternity; it is impossible to discover its beginning. Rebirth, according to Buddhist tradition, follows five possible destinies—hell, animals, spirits, men, and gods—in three different worlds. First comes the world of desire, where the five senses comprise most destinies, those of hell, animals, spirits, men, and some of the gods. Then there is the world of subtle nature or of pure form which comprises celestial beings reborn in the world of Brahma and scattered through the spheres of the four ecstasies (*dyana*). Finally, there is the immaterial world or, beyond the world of form, the world of beings reborn in the spheres of the four meditations; the place where space is infinite, where knowledge is infinite, the place of nothingness, and ultimately where there is neither consciousness nor unconsciousness.

The preaching and practice of Buddha lasted forty years. He travelled all through the valley of the Ganges, returned several times to Kapilavastu where he converted his father, wife, and son, and founded a monastic community but never became its head. Buddha effaced himself before the law he had discovered and only considered himself its servant and in no way divine.

Sakyamuni shows the path and cannot help those who cannot follow it.

About 483 BC Buddha fell ill at the age of 80 and predicted his imminent death. He ate a dish of pork and caught dysentery. He went to Kusinagara and rose to Nirvana. His body was burnt, and the remains were scattered in ten directions: eight consisted of ashes, the ninth consisted of the urn, and the tenth, the cinders of the fire. Over each of these parts, which were carried away by believers, a stupa was erected.

Nirvana presents a double aspect. It is first of all the suppression of all desire and then the end of pain and of all existence. This moral perfection cannot be attained in one terrestrial life and many previous lives have to be lived through. The gesture so often shown of taking the earth as witness (the right hand pointing down to the earth) symbolizes the long preparation necessary and which has the earth as witness at each rebirth. This perfection is expressed not only morally but also by an invisible and glorified body for the contemporaries of Sakyamuni. When the sculptors sought a physical portrayal of the Buddha, they did not try to find a likeness to the historical person but showed his glorified body based on the list of marks by which one recognizes the Buddha. These lists have reference to a young child because that is what the astrologers had in mind; this explains the curious proportions of some statues.

Soon after Buddhism's initial successes, there was a movement to elaborate the doctrine. About 100 BC a text, the *Prajnaparamita*, which can be translated as 'Transcendental Wisdom', was compiled. It forms the kernel of the new doctrine, Mahayana or the Greater Vehicle. Its followers derisively called the old school Hinayana, or Lesser Vehicle.

Mahayana originated for the most part in a sect whose doctrinal texts have been almost entirely destroyed, the *Mahasanghika*, which developed in the Magada in the north of India and also around Amaravati in southern India. According to Conze, the two key words of Mahayana are 'Bodhisattva' and 'void'. The Bodhisattva is a being who wants to become a Buddha. In this way, Siddartha before his illumination was a

Bodhisattva. The big difference between the saints of the Lesser Vehicle and the future Buddhas of the Greater Vehicle is that the latter do not only seek to attain Nirvana for themselves, but also want to be instrumental in helping others to escape from pain. This concept led to the identification of the sovereign with a Bodhisattva assuring the well-being of his kingdom. However, the ideal of future Buddhas is not only compassion. They still have to see, in their infinite wisdom, that all things are empty. Buddhism is not troubled by this contradiction: the Bodhisattva wishes to save beings who are only outward forms. In the Buddhist void, which is the only ultimate reality, there is no duality; the object does not differ from the subject, nor does Nirvana differ from the world, nor does being differ from non-being.

The Greater, like the Lesser, Vehicle only envisages salvation at some remote future time. Even if Mahayana shortens this period of time, the number of rebirths before reaching Nirvana is still considerable. So there is recourse to magic, rituals, formulae, gymnastics, and breath control to speed the path to Buddhahood. These techniques, which are not only Buddhist, form the Tantra and are divided into two groups: the Tantra of the right hand, which upholds the masculine principle of creative energy, and that of the left hand, which emphasizes above all the female principles. In Buddhism, the Tantra of the left hand constitutes the Vajrayana school which began about the year AD 300 in the north of India.

Tantric Buddhism stresses an important mythology which rests on the five Jinas (which are also called, as noted above, the Dhyani Buddhas): Vairocana, the illuminated or the brilliant one; Aksobhya, the imperturbable one; Ratnasambhava, issued from a jewel; Amithaba, infinite light, and Amoghasida, eternal success. These five Buddhas are not ordinary Buddhas who have reached their state through numerous rebirths; they are Buddhas of all eternity, having never been anything else, and comprise the body of the Universe. Each one is mirrored in a celestial Bodhisattva and in a terrestrial Buddha and rules over a whole family of lesser celestial beings.

9

Early Buddhism was strictly masculine, and the female sex was an obstacle to supreme realization. So when the disciple Ananda asked the Buddha, 'How should we behave to women?' the master replied, 'Do not see them.' 'But what if we should see them?' 'Do not speak to them.' 'And if we have to speak to them?' 'Control your thoughts.' But with Tantrism a cult of female divinities spread, especially of Prajnaparamita, which is not only a text but a goddess, and Tara, who aids the believer to cross obstacles separating him from salvation.

The main rites practised by Buddhists are centred on the monastic community which is given alms. The monk must receive any gift, from the humblest to the most magnificent, in the same way. One of the Buddhist saints did not reject a finger which had fallen off a leper into his begging bowl. In principle, each monastery, in addition to the necessary buildings for the material life of the community, such as cells, a dining hall, and a meeting room, includes a sanctuary containing statues, but the most characteristic monument of Buddhism to be found in a monastery is the stupa. Initially, this was doubtless conceived as a reliquary; the placing of relics symbolically gives life to a monument. Gradually, the stupa came to be a major symbol in itself. One of the essential rites of the Buddhist community is linked to the stupa, and this is the *pradakshina*, which consists in moving around the structure keeping it always on the right hand. Another pious obligation for the believer is the beautification and enrichment of the sanctuary. This was principally accomplished by Javanese Buddhists by means of numerous inscriptions, in particular at Candi Plaosan. These preserve the memory of foundations created by the senior officials of the kingdom who had small sanctuaries built around those of the reigning prince near the principal sanctuary.

Buddhism appeared in the Indonesian archipelago in all probability in the early centuries of the Christian era: a bronze Buddha recalling the Amaravati styles of the fourth to the fifth century was found at Sempaga in Sulawesi (Celebes). There was no apparent transition between a neolithic civilization and conversion to Buddhism. Another statue of the Buddha, being closer to those from Ceylon of the fourth to the sixth century, was discovered at Jember in East Java. This and other evidence is too fragmentary for any deduction as to the form of Buddhism practised at the time. However, it was probably the Lesser Vehicle, for in the middle of the seventh century, a Chinese pilgrim, Houi Ning, settled in Java and translated into Chinese the Hinayanist Sanskrit texts. Mahayana appeared in the Malay peninsula where inscriptions of the fifth or sixth century carried Mahayanist lines. The expansion of the Greater Vehicle into the islands took place at the beginning of the eighth century under the influence of the University of Nalanda in Bengal, and it was supported by the Pala dynasty which was then reigning there. This source is not the only one. One can find Sinhalese influence in an inscription discovered at Ratu Boko, near Prambanan, dated 792. Mention is made in this text of a monastery called Abhayagiri Vihara very similar to the name of the famous monastery of Anuradhapura, the old capital of Ceylon. The form of Buddhism mentioned in the Ratu Boko inscription is Mahayanist. De Casparis translated it and thought that monks were banished from their monastery because of Mahayanist doctrinal deviation at the time of the Hinayanist re-establishment in Anuradhapura, and that they are directly the cause of the Abhayagiri Vihara in Java. Nevertheless, de Casparis notes that the Sinhalese chronicles do not mention the expulsion of monks in the second half of the eighth century. Mahayana was found in Ceylon at the end of the sixth century since a copper plaque citing texts of the Greater Vehicle was discovered in the Vijayarama stupa at Anuradhapura.

It can be seen that it is difficult to discover the exact part of India from which Javanese Buddhism came as there were many possible sources and once established there Buddhism evolved in its own way. This is apparent in the *Sang Hyang Kamahaya-nikan*, the oldest parts of which were written in the first half of the tenth century. It is usually agreed that the Buddhism described in this text must be close to the form practised in Borobudur.

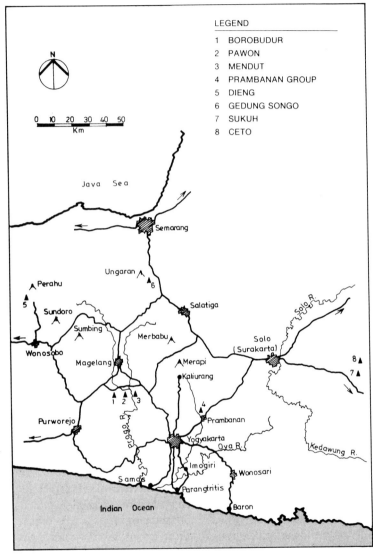

LEGEND

1 BOROBUDUR
2 PAWON
3 MENDUT
4 PRAMBANAN GROUP
5 DIENG
6 GEDUNG SONGO
7 SUKUH
8 CETO

Figure 2. Borobudur and its surroundings. (From Michael Smithies, *Yogyakarta: Cultural Heart of Indonesia*, Singapore, 1986.)

3
The Architectural Setting

THE architectural setting in which Borobudur was created has almost entirely disappeared. There remain, however, three sources of information about it; first, contemporary or earlier monuments which still exist today, secondly, the architectural illustrations on the bas-reliefs of Borobudur and, thirdly, architectural treatises in Sanskrit.

Earlier or Contemporary Monuments

The monuments built before or at the same time as Borobudur are few and mostly Hindu. Because of this, they are different in type and designed for different rites. However, they present, both technically and decoratively, some interesting points of comparison. Those which can be dated epigraphically will be considered first.

An inscription dating from 732 commemorating the erection of a linga on a mountain by King Sanjaya has been discovered on Gunung Wukir, a hill near the road from Yogyakarta to Borobudur. Part of the stele was found in a shrine, Candi Cangal, and another part a little further up the hill. It is generally agreed that the temple mentioned in the stele and Candi Cangal are the same. The temple consists of a main sanctuary, now almost entirely destroyed, surrounded by three small sanctuaries. These consist of a base with a balustrade surrounding a statue raised on a pedestal in the open air.

The next monument chronologically is Candi Kalasan, located in the village of the same name between Prambanan and Yogyakarta. A stele discovered near the present temple dates from 778 and commemorates the construction of the Buddhist temple dedicated to the goddess Tara. The temple as it is now is not the original building, but a third construction, completely covering the first two. However, something is known about the original building, since archaeologists have uncovered the base of the first monument under the north-west corner of the present building (A in Figure 6). Two other Buddhist monuments can be linked with original inscriptions. First, near Prambanan, Candi Lumbung, usually associated with the stele of Kelurak, dating from 782, celebrates the erection of a statue to Manjusri, a distant future Buddha. Then there is Candi Sewu, near Candi Lumbung and Prambanan. An inscription dating from 792 was found on the site. It is probable that this inscription, which is very difficult to read and to translate, only concerns an enlargement of the temple. Candi Sewu has been shown to be a mandala in relief, particularly the Vajradhatu mandala. This temple comprises a main sanctuary surrounded by 240 small sanctuaries.

Other monuments can be associated with undated inscriptions but they can be linked to the others. This is the case with the small Hindu sanctuaries on the Dieng plateau which can be associated with ancient inscriptions that can still be seen on the plateau. Some of them are written in an alphabet very close to that used by the Pallava dynasty (of the middle of the seventh century) which reigned in southern India on the east coast. Other written inscriptions in different scripts are dated, the most recent being 1210. This shows that there was, for five centuries, a great deal of religious activity on the plateau, but it does nothing to help date precisely the different temples. It is generally agreed that the earlier date is correct. The monuments are grouped into two styles, the 'old Dieng style' (roughly 680 to 730) which includes the sanctuaries Arjuna, Semar, Srikandi, and Gatotkaca and the 'new Dieng style' (roughly 730 to 780), with the sanctuaries Puntadewa, Sembodro, and Bima. Bima is the only one which shows a technical change in its construction. The old style is very sober and the newer style is more elaborate, though the ensemble remains extremely homogeneous.

Lastly, some buildings can be linked to earlier constructions

by their style. This is true of the Hindu temples of Gedong
Songo near Ungaran. In the same area are the six small Hindu
temples of Candi Muncul, and these can also be linked to
Dieng.

About 2 km off the main road between Yogyakarta and
Kalasan is the village of Sambisari, in which the Hindu temple
of the same name is found. It is a temple with a similar plan to
that of Candi Cangal, but the building is probably a little later.
The temple was covered with a very substantial layer of rubble,
probably as a result of a flood. This means that it was found
intact. The central sanctuary is raised on a terrace surrounded
by a balustrade; the cella contained a plinth which covered the
foundation well. Archaeologists digging at the site have noticed
that some of the statuary had been altered in the past, either
because of a change in ritual or else to update the building.
There are only three flanking shrines which consist of a small
terrace enclosed by a balustrade interrupted by an entrance
porch on one side. In the centre of each terrace there was a
statue unprotected by any covering structure.

Architectural Illustrations

The architectural illustrations on the bas-reliefs at Borobudur
are extensive. They show in a very uneven way an idealization
of architecture at the time the monument was being built. Only
a few examples will be mentioned here, but this documentation
has considerable detail and interest.

These representations can be divided into two groups,
depending on the main material used, wood or stone. Wooden
architecture is more frequently illustrated, with numerous
technical details which allow us to reconstruct for the most part
a wooden building contemporary with Borobudur. It can be
seen that if stone constructions were in part inspired by Indian
priests, this is also true of wooden architecture, but in the case
of the latter such inspiration is purely formal. However, an
influence of Chinese techniques can be distinguished in some

buildings. Several centuries before the beginning of the Christian era, the so-called Dong-Son civilization spread as far as Indonesia, bringing bronze-casting techniques. But these techniques were perhaps not sufficiently well assimilated for the making of large bronze drums in the area. Associated with many of these bronze drums, a cowrie receptacle dating from the beginning of the Christian era was discovered in an archaeological site in southern China. The cover of this piece is decorated with an architectural illustration on the round bosse. It consists of a house with a roof where the ridge beam is extended by two components at the ends in the form of projecting gables. This very special technique, still used today in Sumatra and Sulawesi, appears on the reliefs of Borobudur, in particular in the lower level on the first gallery, north side, west wing (A in Figure 3).

Mention has already been made of the ancient inscriptions often written in a script similar to that used by the Pallava dynasty. This Pallava influence can be seen again in the architectural illustrations, in particular in a relief located on the first gallery, east side, south wing (B in Figure 3). No contemporary wooden architecture of the Pallavas remains in India but the stone temples comprise numerous elements imitating woodwork, resting on stone pillars, figuring lions standing on their hind legs. This last motif is found on the bas-reliefs. The lions seem to support sections of wooden columns, crowned with capitals that maintain a complete system of beams independent of the building proper.

Masonry buildings are shown with the same attention to detail. The essential monument of the Buddhist religion, the stupa, is often carved on the reliefs (see C, D, E, and F in Figure 3). Its form is said to derive from the following legend. A king asked his architect what form he intended to give to the stupa he was about to construct. The divine architect, Visvakarman, inspired the master craftsman who filled a gold vase with water. He took some water in the hollow of his hand and then threw it hard on to the water still inside the vase. A large

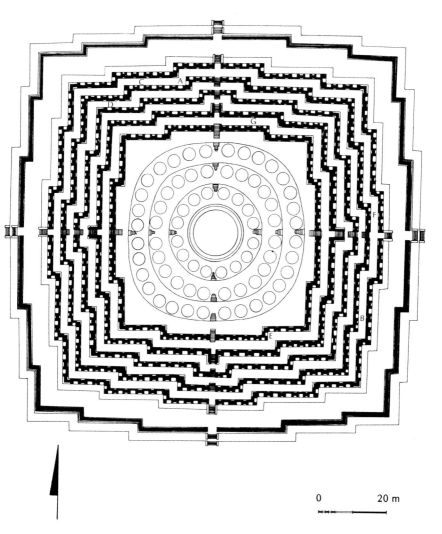

Figure 3. Borobudur.

bubble like a crystal ball was formed. 'That is how I shall do it,' the architect is said to have declared.

This legend and its various moral and cosmogonic inter-pretations explain the different forms of the stupa, which can be almost spherical (C in Figure 3) or alternatively squat (D in Figure 3). Most frequently, it is shown as a flattened half-dome resting on a cylindrical drum (E and F in Figure 3); this is the form of the central stupa at Borobudur but the silhouette of the pierced stupas on the circular terraces does not appear in the bas-reliefs.

Some temples are also shown in these reliefs. Their religious persuasion can be seen from the decoration on the top of the roof. Buddhist temples are capped with stupas and Sivaite temples with a trident. In the fourth gallery, north side, west wing (G in Figure 3) can be seen two temples situated next to each other; one is Sivaite and the other Buddhist. The form of these two buildings can be compared to Candi Arjuna in Dieng.

Architectural Treatises

We mentioned that the Hinduization of the archipelago was brought about by priests. Their influence is shown not only in the ritual necessities required of the architecture and in the symbolism of the monuments, but also in the purely archi-tectural part of the temples, which was possible through the architectural treatises brought by the priests. Comparisons between the texts and the temples have been attempted, in particular between the *Manasara* and the temples in Dieng, and between the siting of Borobudur and the methods proposed in the *Manasara*. But none of these studies is very conclusive, because the texts do not allow for an exact juxtaposition with the architecture. They are not really architectural treatises but rather notes, and for the most part are strictly formal. But in these very dense texts appear technical formulae, the ritual importance of which is underlined. So that in the *Mayamata*, in the chapter dealing with the cutting of lingas, it is stated that

18

one of the sides of the stone must be marked so that the linga will be raised in the same position as that in which the stone was found before its extraction from the quarry. This injunction was not strictly followed.

For the establishment of the foundations, where the ritual importance is very great, the temple must face a clearly determined direction. This requires that the cardinal points be defined in a very exact manner. The *Manasara* proposes the following method: a stake (a gnomon) is fixed vertically in the earth, and taking the base of the stake as the centre, a circle is drawn whose radius is equal to the height of the stake. In the morning, when the shadow of the top of the stake touches the circle, the point is marked and in the evening, when the shadow touches another point on the circle, the same thing is done. These two points clearly indicate the east–west direction. Other marks allow one to build more or less exactly the main geometric forms, though some buildings proposed are absurd and those the least useful as far as the architecture is concerned are included. The authors of these texts seem to try, like lawyers, to anticipate as many problems as possible. This is particularly true of the cornice for which a very large number of mouldings is suggested, but in this considerable mass only a few examples were followed, and very freely at that, because in general only the height of the moulding is indicated without the depth. A large part of the text is lyrical and serves only to bolster the imagination of the master builder.

The architectural setting in Java at the time of the construction of Borobudur was influenced by two movements. One was popular, and most of the houses were built under this influence, using wood almost exclusively. This movement received few outside influences, except for the probably very old Chinese influences in the matter of beam-laying and, more recently, tiling, which seems to be contemporary with the Tang dynasty. The other movement led to a learned kind of architecture with numerous outside influences which are essentially formal. The materials used were wood and stone or brick. The construction techniques were often local inventions with very few foreign influences. However, there are some original Sinhalese techniques in so far as stone cutting is concerned. But the effort required in the construction of such huge ensembles as Candi Sewu and Borobudur brought about much progress, with techniques being exported to Cambodia and then to India. The formal influence is, however, important. Essentially, it probably comes from southern India and appears in the cornice and the pillars of wooden temples. However, there was no direct transposition. For example, the pillars in the shape of a lion, of Pallava origin, are linked with wooden structures which do not seem to relate with what is known of Pallava beamwork.

When Borobudur was begun, Candi Sewu was a builders' yard, Candi Kalasan was in its second period of construction, and the temples mentioned above were quite new. Borobudur was thus created in an architectural setting of great artistic wealth and in full evolution.

4
The Architecture of the Monument

THE site chosen for the construction of Borobudur was doubt-less selected for several reasons. The first of these would be human. It was necessary to construct a building of this import-ance in an area with plentiful labour. It is therefore probable that indirectly the fertility of the River Progo basin played a part in attracting a fairly large population. The religious condi-tions also had to be such as to permit the construction of a Buddhist foundation. (In spite of the considerable tolerance of Hinduism, it is difficult to conceive of such a signal manifesta-tion of Buddhism in an essentially Sivaite environment.) The site may have been selected in relation to existing Buddhist communities. A stele has been found at Kalasan dating from 778, erected in commemoration of the founding of a temple to Tara, and when the Dutch restorers started to clear Candi Mendut, they discovered that it was built over an older brick building. The first Mendut was doubtless already Buddhist and existed before Borobudur. Near the foundations of Borobudur a number of brick funerary stupas has been excavated, and what appears to be the remains of a similar stupa has been discovered from a boring carried out on the side of the hill beneath the monument in deposits formed by stone waste coming from the construction of the monument. Still embodying a fragment of human hip bone, the brick casing was in all respects similar to the bricks at Mendut. However, this stupa must have been relatively close to the period of the construction of Borobudur. But, as many of the monuments in the area were Sivaite, and as the plan of Borobudur is closer to, though on a much larger scale than, contemporary Sivaite buildings, it seems quite possible it was originally conceived as a Hindu shrine on a vast scale.

The monument is sited at the junction of two rivers, the Elo and the Progo, doubtless to evoke the most sacred confluence of all, that of the Ganga (Ganges) and the Yamuna (Jumna). The desire to seek a replica of the holy places of India was not particular to Java. The need for an ideal Buddhist geographical site led, in Angkor, to the construction of the temple of Neak Phean, representing the source of the holy rivers of India. It is therefore possible that, in a similar way, the proximity of the confluence of the two rivers helped to determine the choice of the site. The existence, to the north-east of the monument near present-day Magelang, of the hill known as Tidar, the head of the nail which fixed Java in the sea, also perhaps played a part.

Geologically, the hill consists of volcanic tuff which is weathered on the surface to form a variable thickness of yellow clay. This soil is not very suitable for building operations and contained hollows with projecting rocks. The first thing which had to be done was to level the site. The natural soil was covered with a layer of brown clay. After these preparations, the overseers proceeded to their first pegging out of the ground. The monument is not placed in the centre of the plateau but is slightly to the west, leaving a broad space to the east. It is, furthermore not sited exactly between the northern and southern sides of the plateau, as the space to the north is notably bigger. This last particularity was certainly due to the configuration of the original site which is much more sloping to the south than to the north and, consequently, the monument could not be centred exactly.

The First Period of Construction

On the first marking out, a small wall of three or some-times four carefully edged courses formed the foundations of Borobudur in its first form. As will be seen, the outer foundations were relaid on two occasions. The foundation wall was partly covered by debris from waste stone. The stone used throughout the monument is andesite, most likely collected in the nearby rivers where different volcanic eruptions had carried down large quantities of variously shaped rocks. After the completion of the foundation wall, the next step was the definitive foot which was somewhat set off from the foundation wall. The two foundation lines have several differences between them. The projection is 16 cm on the north-east corner while it is only 8 cm on the south-west, doubtless caused by correcting errors from the first foundations. The sides of the temple are perfectly oriented. The means used to fix the cardinal points are not known but the foundation was probably done from the two perpendicularly oriented axes, on which were drawn perpendicular lines. At the cross point of these the corners of the monument were sited.

As the building progressed, a scaffolding became necessary. It was put into position above the first level of stone waste and the feet of the poles became gradually buried by refuse from the construction. When the walkways began to be paved, the scaffolding remained in place for some time, doubtless until the monument reached the level of the first gallery. At this point, the scaffolding was taken away and the space previously occupied by the poles was filled with stone blocks. The beginning of this construction work was not without technical troubles. After laying the first course of the retaining wall for the second gallery, a major subsidence occurred on the west side, doubtless because the fill had been badly compacted. It became necessary to realign the level of the base of the wall-facing with a levelling course of wedge-shaped stones.

At the level of the third gallery, a structure was built about which little is known. It was probably almost completed, the proportions and cornice outline and the reliefs mostly begun, before it was completely destroyed. The existence of this structure is known through two facts. According to the borings made for geological research, there emerges at the level of the third gallery inside the monument a relatively narrow area where the infill was very tightly compacted, indicating a working area which must have been in use for some time. Secondly, under the big north stairway which gave on to the foot of the monument and dating from the second period of construction, a large number of carved architectural elements, including cornices and pinnacles, have been discovered. All this debris did not belong to the present building, even though it came from a building whose outline was very similar. There existed, then, at the end of the first period of construction a complete monument which included a foot which is now hidden, the two first galleries, and a central structure since destroyed. The sides of the hill were doubtless arranged in steps which must have been interrupted on each of the axes by the stairways, the siting of which had been laid out but the masonry work not yet begun.

The monument remained in this state a fairly short time, probably less than twenty-five years, because, apart from the well-compacted surface layer, the infill was not yet stabilized and subsidence began. This may have been the cause of the resumption of the work.

The Second Period of Construction

The earth movement is especially noticeable on the north side of the monument. The layer of stone debris slipped and a large gully appeared in the hillside. This is why, quite naturally, the supervisor decided not to use the parts of the structure destroyed on the northern side. This second period of construction was a complete renewal of the building, while seeking to keep its unity. However, the new plan for the third and fourth galleries shows slight differences. The stairways had to be reconstructed as the structure of the first period was lower and consequently the stairways were less steep. For the new plan, it was necessary to redesign them and to rebuild the arches that covered the entrances which no longer gave access to the galleries. To give a unity to the monument, new entrance jambs were put on to the old reliefs which were similar to those on the third and fourth galleries.

At the same time, work was resumed at the base of the monument. A massive foot completely obliterated the reliefs of the first period and on the sides of the hill a complex grading was begun which included five levels of compressed earth covering the layers of debris that had been produced by demolition and construction. These levels were interrupted to give room for the stone stairways partially raised above each levelling, disclosing the string-walls which were then dressed with stone where they were exposed.

The levels were laid out following the layout of the monument in relation to the hill, leaving a large area to the east as in the previous period of construction. This space was still further enlarged by a broad projection on each side of the east stairway. It is not known how these levels ended on the north-west corner where the monument joins the prolongation of the hill. While a fairly large circular structure was being built on the top platform, the work was again interrupted.

The Third Period of Construction

It is not known in what state the builders of the second period left the central structure but it is likely that before new construction work was begun it was levelled before proceeding to the new structure, doubtless utilizing the concave elements of the upper part of the moulded base of the second stage. The work of this period included the construction of the three approximately circular terraces, the pierced stupas, and the central stupa. At the same period, the balustrade of the first gallery was modified by constructing niches on the curved moulding of the top of the balustrade to add to the number of Buddhas, as will be seen below. At the base of the monument the foot was given further attention by extending the first level and inserting gutters to remove rain water to the edge of the earth platform. It would seem that these gutters were extended eastwards along the length of the steps which had been begun to be dressed on the eastern side. This enormous job was only done in outline, though the two upper levels of the east side on the north wing were completed.

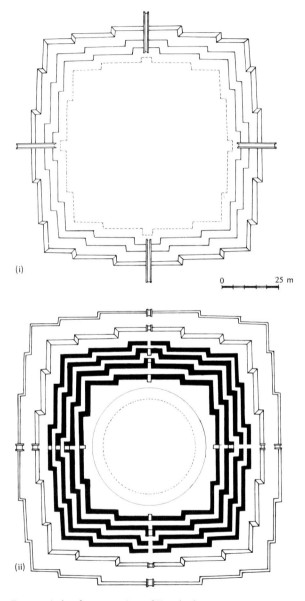

(i)

0   25 m

(ii)

Figure 4. Four periods of construction of Borobudur.

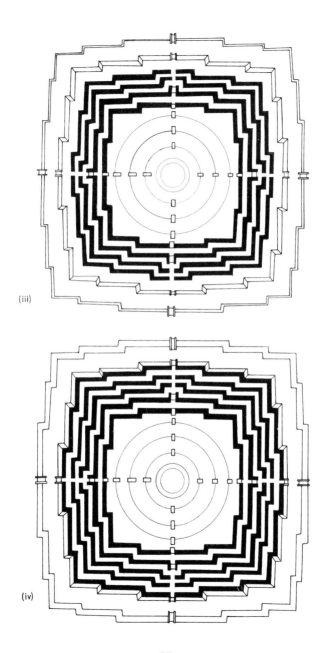

(iii)

(iv)

The Fourth and Fifth Periods of Construction

These two last periods of construction were simply improvements to the monument in the course of its existence and, in contrast with the previous periods, did not modify its plan. They included blocking the space between the open niches on the balustrade of the first gallery, and the insertion of a new series of reliefs on the inside of the first gallery under the moulded top of the balustrade. These reliefs were linked with new entrance doorways and new access stairways inserted after a fashion into the previous structures. At this time, the compacted earth steps on the hillsides eroded and the debris fell down the slopes except on the eastern side which was always better maintained.

Even if the monument continued to be visited for some time, the construction work ceased and the upkeep became ever more neglected. Earth accumulated along the length of the monument to the point of covering the whole of the first level of the foot. The steps and the stairways in the sides of the hill disappeared completely. The galleries progressively filled with earth and vegetation invaded the structures which remained visible. Borobudur started its lengthy sleep.

The Techniques of Construction

The construction, with these numerous stops and starts, lasted a period thought to be about seventy-five years. During such a length of time, the techniques did not remain unchanged and several modifications in the methods used can be seen. However, in essence, it is a homogeneous construction of stone put together without mortar. Cohesion was consequently obtained internally, using different cuttings to ensure the strength of the building.

Two main types of joints have been noted and they have several variants. The first is a system using right angles, either on the vertical or the horizontal plane. If there were movement the right angles locked into each other, and made for excellent cohesion. In this way, whole panels can be seen as having shifted all in one piece. Sometimes, especially in the paving, the right angles were locked into each other with the aid of a forcibly inserted wedge. This last method, probably of Sinhalese origin, only appeared in Java in the second half of the eighth century, that is, a short time before the beginning of the work on Borobudur. Secondly, a technique using tenons which gripped the mortices was used, but this was only used on the monument from the time of the second period of construction.

The stones were linked to each other by double dovetailed clamps. This was not very efficient as the clamps were hewn from the same material, which is quite fragile when fairly thin. In Cambodia, in the same manner, clamps were used to bind the stones but they were generally of metal. The stairways were covered with a cantilever arch, held at the top by a T-shaped keystone which stays on the last course of the corbelling and goes below the upper level of the course, so assuring a good coherence to the cantilever even when there is movement.

The sculpture was begun *in situ* when the structure was completed. Several unfinished panels give an indication of the techniques used by the sculptors. On appropriately smooth stone, the design was marked out with a chasing chisel and the parts which were to constitute the background were begun first, leaving in relief somewhat convex volumes. Then the sculptor took up the surface again, doing the figures in the foreground and finally the decoration which always remains relative to the attention given to the figures. Finally, the whole was covered with stucco which was a simple mortar of lime and sand. Although this stucco at Borobudur has completely disappeared, apart from a few very rare places, this is not so at Candi Kalasan where it may still be studied. The stucco covering on this monument comprises two superimposed layers, consisting of the same mixture in the same proportions of lime and the same granule consistency of sand. The first layer is thought to have contained the porosity of the andesite and the second layer could then be moulded more easily since the water used for the composition was not absorbed by the stone. Thus the mortar stayed malleable longer. Doubtless the sculptor touched up the figures once the stucco was completed, which would explain why sometimes the stone carving is only sketched in. It is not known if the monument was painted but it seems likely. The reliefs of the major Khmer monuments, for instance, were painted in fairly bright colours of blue, red, green, and black, enhanced by the application of gold leaf.

The Architecture of the Monument

As has been shown, there was no unity of conception to Borobudur and the present state of the monument is an adaptation of an old idea to a new design. Thus visitors are usually struck by the starkness of the circular terraces which contrasts with the wealth of decoration of the quadrangular galleries. One can see the desire of the supervisors of the third stage of construction to break with what had been initially envisaged at the second stage, namely an outline as rich as the base. The symbolism of the monument cannot therefore be presented as a sort of cosmogony where every detail was considered in advance. On the contrary, it would appear that each stage of construction was conceived with a different symbolism.

The description here is of the monument at its peak, that is to say, at the end of the third stage of construction when its setting was still intact. The approach to Borobudur was from the east and was without doubt along a path which started at Candi Mendut. This path crossed the River Elo and then led to the edge of the Progo where a small construction existed of which only a few brick elements remain. One crossed the river and Candi Pawon marked a new stage. These buildings are perhaps only parts of a much larger whole surrounding Borobudur with a chain of small temples. The few remains of Wringin Putih, 2 km from the north-west corner, may support such a hypothesis. The main entrance was thus from the east. Indeed, it has already been noted that the monument was shifted fairly markedly to the west on a terrace reached by a vast stairway 4 m wide (the steps were fairly steep, being

22 cm high with a depth of 25 cm). The starting point for the east stairway has, unfortunately, entirely disappeared but a similar stairway was constructed on each of the axes of the monument and the point of departure of the north stairway has been relatively well-preserved. It consisted of a small platform composed of rough ashlar supporting a paving decorated with lions. The variations in level between this platform and the terrace differed according to the axes and brought about modifications in the width of the stairways. The longest extension is to the south where the drop is 12 m, while it is only 7 m to the west and 10 m to the north.

The importance of the variation in level of the southern stairway, which ends at the side of a fairly large depression, has given rise to the idea that this could have been a pool. However, a study has shown that the vegetation found in the lower depths of the depression was not aquatic. It is possible this space was one of the sources of the fill.

All the steps of the stairways are of stone and rest on rough ashlar lying on a layer of sand and the debris of stone cutting. The east stairway is bordered by steps projecting from the terrace alignment which is crossed by four paved paths constructed in the same way as the stairways. These paths lead to the base of the monument proper, the foot of which is not strictly symmetrical. The northern half is slightly larger than the southern half but the differences are slight. It is thought that the displacement to the north was introduced in the second construction stage. The first gallery is completely symmetrical, but when the new foot was added, it followed a new base line with a slight displacement to the north of 20 cm. If these variations are not great, it is because the new construction had to be incorporated in an older structure, and it can be seen that the supervisor of the second stage, when he was freed from the constraints imposed by the walls of his predecessors, noticeably increased the dissymmetry. The retaining wall of the last terrace is off course by 50 cm to the north, which is similar to the shift in some Khmer temples (40 cm at Ta Kev and 43 cm at the Bayon). The circular terraces were approximately centred on the last quadrangular platform. This caused the axes of the stairways to be displaced and they are not in the prolongation of the entries leading from the galleries.

The monument is only a framework for the sculpture. It is essentially a carved ensemble and architectural values play a minor role. This is reflected in the techniques of construction which seek to give coherence and to find the form of the original stone. However, the purely architectural difficulties of movement of people, the time it takes to go round, and the removal of rainwater played a part in the composition independently of all symbolism. The problem for the different supervisors was that they had to spread the reliefs to the length required by the illustration of the text and one had to read the text. The galleries, therefore, had to be sufficiently wide so that a panel in relief could be seen at one glance. This decided the width of the gallery and in some degree its development. Some of the panels may be considered as padding. One could maintain, for instance, that in spite of the beauty of the carving, the scene of Queen Maya's journey to the Lumbini garden is not essential to an understanding of a visual illustration of the life of the Buddha. Without such scenes, however, the continuity of the gallery would otherwise have been difficult to arrange. The reading of the reliefs was done from the east, keeping the monument to the right. When the reading of one gallery is completed, one is back to the beginning. Only one stairway, the eastern one, is used to go up. This stairway must have been somewhat crowded when there were many pilgrims. The galleries become increasingly narrow as one goes higher, which implies that either the upper galleries were crowded or that one moved more quickly as one got near the top. The platform supporting the circular terraces probably served as a clearing space for visitors and it is thought its huge dimensions have perhaps no other reason. One went down by any stairway, undoubtedly avoiding the eastern one which was crowded with people going up. The stairway most likely to have been used for going down is the western one, leading to the monastery.

1. Borobudur, string-wall of the first state appearing in the exposed base.

2. Borobudur, north façade, detail.

3. Borobudur, first gallery, east side.

4. Borobudur, first gallery, east side, upper level.

5. Borobudur, second gallery.

6. Borobudur, fourth gallery, north side.

The removal of rainwater was, as has been noted, foreseen at several junctures. The system was very simple. Gargoyles were placed at the diagonals of the monument, bringing the water down from one level to the one below as far as the first gallery, where the water on the foot was collected at the base of the first level in a gutter surrounding the monument. Other gutters took the water to the edge of the earth platform. In spite of the heavy rainfall of 1 800 mm a year, this system remained efficient as long as the monument was stable, but as soon as the first shift in the structure occurred, the gargoyles did not disperse the water. This seeped through the infill and hastened the ruin of the whole.

The Foot

The second foot, which hides the first, comprises two steps of very unequal widths. The lower step is uniformly 2.35 m wide. The upper level, forming a large platform 6.75 m wide, was surrounded by a very low balustrade, pierced at the bottom with a number of openings for the rainwater to flow through. This balustrade is now almost completely destroyed, though a few sizeable parts remain at the north-west corner of the monument. These two levels were interrupted on the four axes by the stairways, sometimes projecting above the level of the structure. Where this is so, they have decorated ramparts on either side. At the top of the rampart where it was flat, a lion's head appeared to disgorge the balustrade which ends at the base either in a spiral scroll or in a Makara head with its open mouth clasping a lion with one paw raised. A richly carved cornice decorates the hidden foot, the plinth of which is decorated with 160 reliefs illustrating the *Karmawibhangga*. This text describes the doctrine of the causes and effects of good and evil. About 40 of these reliefs (the exact number is not known because of the damage caused by the building of the added foot) are topped with a brief description in Old Javanese but written in Sanskrit letters. These inscriptions have been translated. Their meaning is related to the relief but in a very indirect way, for example, 'the evil faces' or 'the offering of the parasol' or 'the banner'. They are sometimes interpreted as being an indication for the sculptor, since in all probability they would have disappeared beneath the stucco. It would seem that these inscriptions are like those in the gallery of the heavens and the hells in Angkor Wat, dating from the twelfth century, which are placed in the middle of the sculpture and were certainly carved after the sculptor had finished his work. These few words may have served as a cue to the person guiding visitors around the stupa. Above the plinth, a broad curved moulding is found, together with other elements culminating in a final upper ledge or torus. In this convex moulding, the concave moulding, or cyma, was inserted, making the link between the added foot and the older structure.

The First Gallery

The first gallery is reached by gateways which have now almost completely disappeared, though a few fragments remain to the east and the south. These gateways were constructed with two carved outer facings and rough infilling, a technique which was only used in Java after the construction of the central temple at Prambanan. They can therefore be dated approximately to the middle of the ninth century, and the construction of the gateways and the sculpture of the reliefs tally with this. The gallery itself comprises the retaining wall of the second gallery and the balustrade stopping the view to the outside. The retaining wall is decorated at two levels with 120 panels each.

The upper level illustrates the *Lalitavistara*, the story of the life of the Buddha from his birth to the sermon at Benares. This series is the most easily understood. Among the numerous panels can be seen the future Buddha, before his birth, in-forming the gods of his intention to return to earth, his conception in the body of Queen Maya, his birth in the garden in Lumbini, his education, the four decisive encounters with

1. Candi Sewu, east façade.

2. Candi Sewu, north façade.

3. Borobudur, north façade.

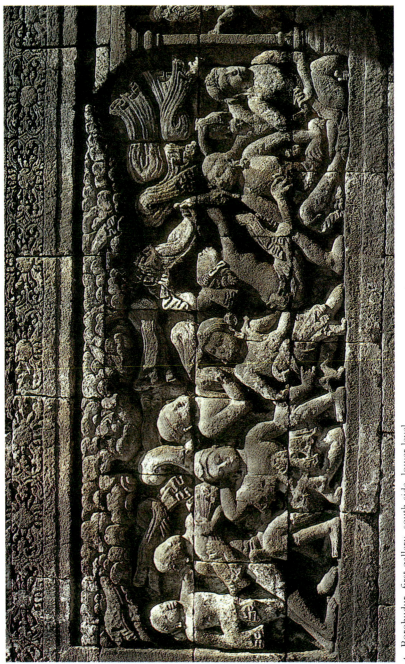

4. Borobudur, first gallery, south side, lower level.

5. Borobudur, first gallery, north side.

6. Borobudur, first gallery, north side, lower level.

7. Borobudur, stairway between the first and second galleries, north side.

8. Borobudur, second gallery.

9. Borobudur, second gallery.

10. Borobudur, third gallery.

11. Borobudur, gargoyle.

12. Borobudur, south façade from the upper level.

13. Borobudur, upper terrace.

14. Borobudur, central stupa.

15. Candi Plaosan, south façade.

16. Borobudur, general view during restoration work.

poverty, illness, death, and asceticism, the great departure, the hair-cutting, the onslaught of the demons of Mara's army, then the temptations of Mara's daughters and, finally, the arrival at Benares and the preaching of the sermon.

The lower level illustrates five episodes in the former lives of the historic Buddha. These tales, the *Jatakamala*, were collected in the fourth century. On the inside face of the balustrade can be seen also two levels of reliefs likewise illustrating previous lives of the Buddha, but in the north-east corner the panels of the upper level illustrate another text, the *Awada*. This collection of tales relates not to the previous lives of the historic Buddha, but to Bodhisattvas. The last two series of reliefs are either found under the curved moulding or on the backs of the niches opening outwards. Each of these contains a seated Buddha whose symbolical gesture is different for each of the four cardinal points: to the east, the Buddha points his right hand down towards the earth, signifying the calling of the earth as witness (*bhumisparshamudra*); to the south, the Buddha's right hand rests on his knee, the open palm expressing charity (*varadamudra*); to the west, the two hands are brought flat together one above the other on the lap, palms upwards, symbolizing meditation (*dhyanamudra*); and to the north, the right hand is raised, expressing fearlessness (*abhayamudra*). The same arrangement can be found on each of the balustrades of the second, third, and fourth galleries. Nevertheless, the number of Buddha statues is different:

First gallery	104 Buddhas
Second gallery	104 Buddhas
Third gallery	88 Buddhas
Fourth gallery	72 Buddhas
	368 Buddhas

On the second, third, and fourth balustrades all the space which could be turned into niches is used, but this is not so for the first gallery where 120 niches could have been placed, though only 104 have been built, doubtless in order to arrive at the precise total of 368. This figure can have many symbolic meanings whereas the number 384 has none.

Externally, under all the niches and the ogee moulding the balustrade is decorated with panels showing feminine deities alternating with groups of apparently demoniac persons.

The Second, Third, and Fourth Galleries

The upper galleries comprise the same elements, the retaining wall of the next level, and a balustrade. The retaining wall, which forms the base of these three galleries, is decorated with a single level of reliefs illustrating, on the second and third galleries, the *Gandawyuha*, considered to be one of the most important Buddhist texts. It describes the search for wisdom by Sudhana, the son of a merchant who wishes to acquire great knowledge and to do so meets a large number of Bodhisattvas among whom can be noted, on the reliefs on the third gallery, the Maitreya, the next Buddha. Naturally, the scenes on all three are very similar, showing Sudhana in conversation with one of his spiritual masters. They are not easily identifiable and the significance of many of the panels remains conjectural. But it is certain that the supervisors in charge of the monument attached much importance to this text. They gave over 488 panels to it, whereas, as has been seen, 120 were enough to illustrate the *Lalitavistara*. The panels on the upper galleries are spread out not only on the retaining wall and the backs of the balustrades of the second and third galleries but also on the balustrade of the fourth gallery. The main wall of the fourth gallery, however, is decorated with 72 panels illustrating another text, the *Bhadratjari*, a kind of long conclusion to the *Gandawyuha*, illustrating the pledge of Sudhana to follow the example of Bodhisattva Samantabhadra. Here again, the interpretation of the panels is not always clear.

On the outer wall, the decoration of these three balustrades shows some differences from that of the first gallery where the niches are topped with pinnacles, whereas those on the other balustrades have stupas.

The Upper Platform and the So-called Circular Terraces

The upper platform is surrounded by a fifth balustrade, plain on the inside but similar to the three previous balustrades on the outside. However, the 64 niches decorating this balustrade contain Buddhas in the same position on all sides, unlike the other balustrades where the position of the Buddhas is different on each side. The right hand of these Buddhas is raised like those of the northern side, but the first finger touches the thumb in a gesture symbolizing reasoning (*vitarkamudra*). This series brings the number of Buddhas to 432.

The first two terraces have pierced stupas and are not strictly circular. They have, rather, the shape of a square with its edges rounded off. However, the third terrace and the great central stupa are perfectly circular. On the first terrace are 32 open-work stupas with lozenge-shaped openings. The plinth of the finial is square. There are 24 similar stupas on the second terrace. The third terrace has 16 stupas which are markedly different: the openings are square and the finial is raised on an octagonal plinth. Each of these 72 stupas contains a Buddha statue, the gesture of which symbolizes the release of the Wheel of the Law during the Benares sermon. The two hands are raised to chest level, the right above the left, with the fourth fingers touching (*dharmachakramudra*). This last series of Buddhas brings the total number to 504.

The main central stupa contains two chambers, one above the other, both empty. At the time of the clearing of the monument in 1842 on the orders of Hartman, the Resident of Kedu, an unfinished statue of the Buddha with the right hand extending down to earth was discovered in an excavation made by treasure hunters. It seems unlikely that this statue came from the lower chamber of the central stupa and may have been left unfinished because it was inconsistent in some way. There are other unfinished statues scattered around the monument on which work was obviously abandoned.

Nevertheless, were the chambers of the central stupa empty? For what reason did the thieves, possibly at the end of the eighteenth century, decide to smash the stupa open? They may have done so as a result of a chance discovery of some precious object in another stupa. There is some slight evidence that the treasure hunters carried off important booty in that they did not carry their investigations further.

Candi Mendut and Candi Pawon

These two monuments are laid out on the same east–west line. The alignment was probably not accidental, in spite of a slight change of direction on the eastern side to towards the north-east (a privileged direction in Indian architecture). The topographical position, as well as the moulding, is similar, though on a different scale, with Borobudur, and shows that they are interrelated.

Mendut was built, according to de Casparis, by King Indra on an older brick structure. The temple is raised on a massive rectangular foundation and consists of a square cella preceded by an entrance portico. The cella contains three statues, with the seated Sakyamuni Buddha in the centre teaching the law. At the bottom of the plinth can be seen the Wheel of the Law flanked by two gazelles, a reference to the sermon preached in the gazelle park in Benares where the Buddha taught the Law for the first time. To the left is the Bodhisattva Avalokitesvara, and to the right another Bodhisattva, probably Manjusri.

The portico underwent some' changes about the middle of the ninth century. The double wallfacing technique was used as in the fifth period in the construction of Borobudur. These changes probably caused the east window above the entrance to the cella to be blocked in.

The outside of the monument is decorated with panels representing Bodhisattvas under parasols. These form part of the Mahayana pantheon, among whom are Manjusri and Samantabhadra, who can also be seen at Borobudur. Nearer to eye level are reliefs decorating the outer sides of the string-walls of the stairway, illustrating classical Indian moralities. On the left-hand side, the fable of the tortoise and the two ducks can easily be seen. La Fontaine, incidentally, knew of this tale from a popular version of the *Pancatantra* which Bernier (whose book of 1670 was one of the earliest Western publications relating to Indian art) had introduced to him. The other fables are not always so easy to identify though some of them have been interpreted as illustrating the previous lives of Buddha.

Pawon was probably built at the same time as Mendut. It is on a square base and contained a single statue resting against the carved projecting part of the west wall of the cella. The restoration of both Pawon and Mendut at the beginning of the twentieth century makes their architectural interpretation difficult, particularly so with the top of Pawon which seems of doubtful authenticity.

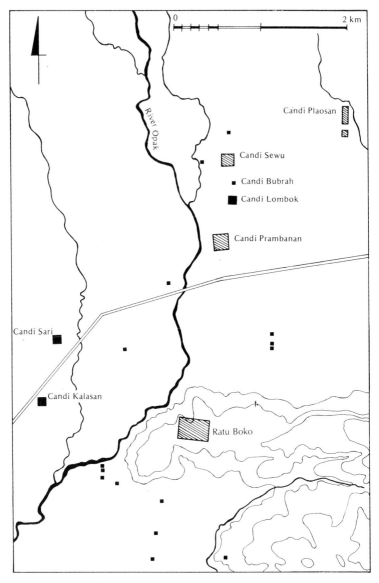

Figure 5. Surroundings of Prambanan.

5
Buddhist Architecture in the Ninth Century

It has been seen that a profound change in the concept of Buddhism very likely took place in Java at the end of the eighth century. Borobudur underwent the important transformations already described, influenced by a text similar to the *Sang Hyang Kamahayanikan*. Bosch has shown that Candi Sewu followed a different tradition, although also associated with Mahayanist Buddhism. He found traces of this concept in Balinese texts and also in Japanese Buddhism. In spite of the considerable differences between Borobudur and Candi Sewu, it would seem that the major modifications carried out on these two temples, as well as on Kalasan, arose from the same doctrinal movement in Mahayanist Buddhism which showed itself in the practical application of a mandala to the temples brought about by the influence of different texts and giving dissimilar results. This new religious impetus was also the reason for the construction of Candi Sari and Candi Plaosan, and it is probably not unrelated to the temples in the second precinct of Prambanan, even though this was a Hindu building.

Candi Kalasan

At the end of the eighth century, the temple was still in its original form, a simple square cella. The transformation of this plan into a cruciform building followed a concept apparently very similar to the one used for the remodelling of Candi Sewu, which is described below. It concerned the modification of a sanctuary which was, to simplify considerably, a shelter for a statue, converting it into a mandala expressing a theogony, an account of the geneology of the gods. This implies finding room for a much greater number of statues which have to be

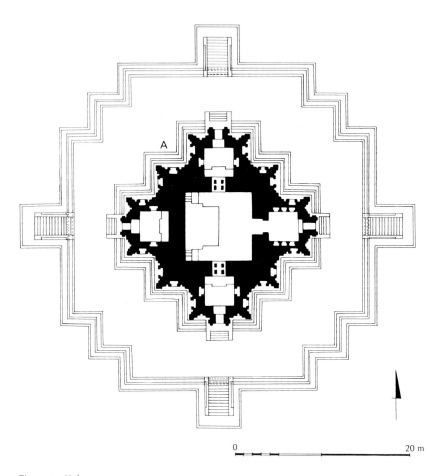

0   20 m

Figure 6. Kalasan.

placed in a given order and accounts for the cruciform arrangement. The second plan was insufficient for this and a third gave
new meaning to the monument. It does not seem to be related
to Candi Sewu, but to the third period of construction at
Borobudur. The capping was transformed and the upper
Buddhas and the niches for them were added. Kalasan, at the
same time, also underwent a general strengthening. The level
of the cella was raised and the base of the central statue
modified. The stucco work, which can still be seen in some
parts, was added in this third period. The two layers of
plastering which can be seen on the masonry do not indicate a
restoration but show the use of a different technique mentioned
in Chapter 4. The statues have disappeared, except for a few
Buddhas on the capping. The statue of the main cella was
probably bronze as the support of the mount has traces of
metallic oxide.

Candi Sewu

Candi Sewu means 'a thousand temples' though, in fact, there
are only 240 small sanctuaries in the second precinct. The term
probably simply indicates a large number. However, it has
been noted that the requirements for the mandala are a thousand secondary sanctuaries. It is likely, therefore, that the
modern name unintentionally restores the original nature of the
monument. The central sanctuary of Candi Sewu is not in its
original state but has undergone a substantial change. In its first
form the building was a simple square cella, surrounded by
four smaller temples without much connection with the main
building. The transformation involved changing the plan to a
cruciform one, by modifying the position of the doorways.
The door-frames (marked S on the plan in Figure 7) were
removed. The passages indicated by the letter O in the plan
were closed by doors whereas they were left open in the first
state of the building, and the doors marked F were narrowed.
In this way it can be seen that the niches cut into the external
dressing of the wall of the central cella were incorporated into

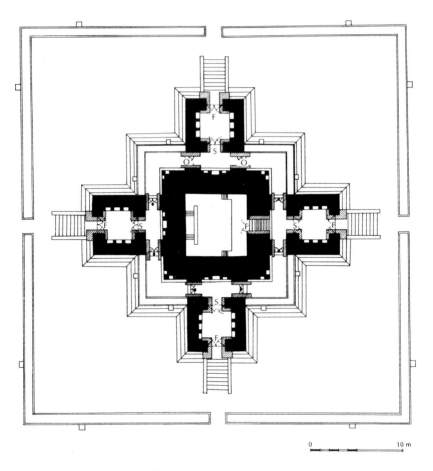

Figure 7. Central sanctuary of Candi Sewu.

the side sanctuaries. It was also during this modification that the 240 small shrines were built inside the second precinct. They all have the same plan, a square cella with a small portico in front, but they are all different in decorative detail and in the arrangement of the statues—almost all of which have disappeared. Those which can be seen on the site are not in their original position. These statues are quite similar, in the way they are made, to those at Borobudur. It seems likely that the main statues were of bronze.

Candi Sewu, as mentioned before, cannot be separated from two smaller monuments nearby, Candi Bubrah and Candi Lumbung. Only the base of Bubrah and the elements of the walls of the cella have survived. On the surface of this base the previous tracing of the axis of the walls can be seen. Candi Lumbung is in a better state of preservation and comprises a central sanctuary surrounded by 16 smaller buildings, rather like those at Candi Sewu. The cella of the central sanctuary is square and opens to the east. The four walls are hollowed out with niches, one to each wall on the south, west, and north but two on the east side, on either side of the entrance. The central niche of the west wall is topped with a much smaller niche. This was probably hidden by the ceiling which rested on the cornice and concealed the inner surface of the vault above.

Candi Sari

The temple of Candi Sari is now reduced to its main sanctuary. It was probably surrounded by buildings and shrines similar to those at Plaosan. It faces east and consists of two levels of three cellas. The upper floor was reached by a wooden staircase located in the south cella (A in Figure 8). The upper cellas were also used for worship and not, as is often repeated by guides, as monks' quarters or a treasury. The statues inside the building have all disappeared. The excellent external decoration consists of female divinities, probably Taras, who are carrying flowers, and of Bodhisattvas with musical instruments, among whom can be seen one playing the lute and another the cymbals. Some

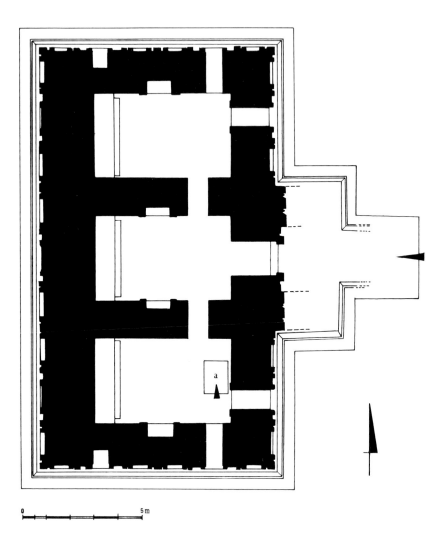

0 ⊢━━━━━━━━━━━━━━┥ 5 m

Figure 8. Candi Sari.

of these Bodhisattvas are associated with the planets; the crescent moon can be seen at the south-west corner.

Candi Plaosan

Candi Plaosan is today completely different and very complex. The two main sanctuaries, on the same plan as Candi Sari but opening to the west, are in the centre of two juxtaposed rectangular precincts. Both of these are enclosed in a courtyard containing 174 small buildings: 116 stupas and 58 shrines. A great number of short inscriptions has been found on these buildings. Two of them mention the gift of a sanctuary by Rakai Pikatan, which allowed de Casparis, who published these texts, to date the gift to between 825 and 850. This date is very close to that of the construction of Prambanan (consecrated in 856). Prambanan was constructed by a new method which is general to the later Hindu-Javanese monuments and this can be seen in Plaosan, in particular in the main building to the north, where two andesite dressings enclose a very indifferent infill of volcanic tuff. Candi Sari, however, is probably earlier. What can be seen of the base is technically very similar to Kalasan.

In the main temples at Plaosan, the cellas on the ground floor each had a bronze statue flanked by two stone statues. The bronze seated statues, with legs folded, rested on a stone base in the form of a lotus and are all missing. The stone statues represent Bodhisattvas and are nearly all in place. Upstairs, it seems likely that there were statues, but because of the arrangement of the windows there was not, as on the ground floor, a group of three statues but probably only one on each altar. The reliefs may well show donors and are found on the inside walls on the ground floor. The traditional representation of a Khmer prince, distinguished by his crown, can be seen in the person carved on the right-hand wall of the northern cella. The divinities on the external walls are not as fine as at Candi Sari and are nearly all male. Only the small personages around the windows are female.

The Meaning of the Buddhist Monuments

Bosch identified the mandala which served as the design of the second period of construction of Candi Sewu as the Vajradhatu mandala. This comprises the five Jinas: Vairocana in the centre, Ratnasambhava in the south, Amithaba in the west, Amoghasida in the north, and Aksobhya in the east. The main problem in linking the Vajradhatu mandala with Candi Sewu lies in the last figure. It is not possible to place a divinity to the east, since it is in the entrance of the portico of the cella in which Vairocana is to be found. So Bosch places the statues representing the Jinas on the right hand on entering the side chapels, and in the niches hollowed into the walls perpendicular to those of the central cella. This does not correspond to the position of the Jinas indicated in the mandala, where they are found along the axes of the central square containing Vairocana. In spite of this caveat, the identification seems likely. To confirm this hypothesis, small statues in bronze have been discovered at Nganjuk in East Java. These certainly form part of a very similar mandala but centred on Manjusri. Aksobhya is to be found there and most of the Taras in the Vajradhatu mandala.

Candi Sari and Plaosan are also mandalas. This is particularly obvious at Plaosan with the small temples in the second precinct. It would seem that the introduction of a second floor in the central buildings of the temples is an architectural expression of Buddhist tantric mythology. In Chapter 2 it was seen that each Jina is linked to an earthly Buddha and a celestial Bodhisattva. The Bodhisattva would be shown on the ground floor and the Buddha above. This is only a theory partly confirmed, however, by the reliefs of Candi Sari where Taras similar to those at Nganjuk are to be found, namely the Tara carrying flowers, and that playing the cymbals. In spite of so many differences, it would seem that these temples are in large part the expression of many forms of the Mahayanist theogony.

However, the additions to Candi Plaosan by the Sanjaya ruler, Rakai Pikatan, probably correspond to something else.

54

This particular mandala would seem to represent the kingdom. De Casparis indicated that the inscriptions should be placed geographically, the dignitaries of the west to the west, those of the south to the south, and so on. The gifts of the kings would occupy a privileged position in the corners or on the axes of the sides. Although this, in the state of current knowledge of the ancient geography of Central Java, is very difficult to prove, it seems very likely. At the end of the first half of the ninth century, not only the temple but the whole kingdom becomes a mandala. One can perhaps see beginning to develop in this identification a political effort on the part of Rakai Pikatan asserting himself over the whole country on becoming free of the Sailendra tutelage. Offering a sanctuary in a temple that represents the kingdom can be seen to be a devout act ensuring merit in the hereafter, and the enrichment of the kingdom itself also becomes a devout act. It is probable that Rakai Pikatan gave expression to a similar idea, but for the consumption of Hindu believers, in constructing the small temples in the second precinct of Prambanan, where de Casparis found some inscriptions in the same geographical disposition as at Plaosan.

This concept of Buddhism, directly adapted to ruling the kingdom, was to be richly illustrated much later at the beginning of the thirteenth century by the Khmer king, Jayavarman VII, who, with the Bayon, constructed an ideal vision of the kingdom centred around his omnipresent personality.

Candi Prambanan

This Sivaite temple, mentioned several times in the text, falls somewhat outside the scope of Borobudur and the Buddhist monuments of Central Java, and is described in detail in *The Temples of Java*. However, it is the most striking manifestation of the Hindu renaissance which took place in Central Java after 832, and appears to have been built between 835 and 856.

It comprises three precincts. The outer one is almost entirely destroyed. Between a second enclosure and the inner wall were 224 small shrines. The inner enclosure contains the main shrine of Candi Siva in the centre, Candi Visnu to the north, and Candi Brahma to the south. All three face east and in front of each was a temple dedicated to the mounts of the gods.

The main buildings are all of cruciform plan, with the central shrine having a corridor to reach the inner cella, in which a huge statue of Siva and not his more common symbol, a linga, is found. The inner side of the balustrade is decorated with carved panels representing scenes from the *Ramayana*.

The verticality of the central shrines in this huge ensemble, representing the cosmic mountain, Mount Meru, is in marked contrast to the horizontal appearance of Borobudur, but numerous architectural devices are common to both. Extensive restoration is currently being carried out at Prambanan.

Kraton Ratu Boko on the hill nearby is also being extensively restored, and seems to have been a palace rather than a shrine, though both Hindu and Buddhist rites appear to have been conducted there.

Candi Sambisari, mentioned in Chapter 3, is another finely preserved Hindu temple, but far more horizontal in appearance. It is found off the road between Yogyakarta and Prambanan, but predates it, being of the eighth century in all probability.

6
Rediscovery and Restoration

AFTER the ninth century, power in Java shifted, for reasons still largely uncertain, to the east of the island. The kingdoms of Kediri, Singosari, and Majapahit were essentially Hindu and most temples, therefore, replicated the cosmic mountain found at Prambanan, if they did not become a series of wooden structures raised on stone or brick platforms, after the model of Candi Sambisari, as at Penataran, a style which continues today in a modified form in Hindu Bali.

Hinduism in Java became more esoteric, as can be seen in the two temples on Mount Lawu, near Solo—Candi Sukuh and Candi Ceto—both of the fifteenth century and the last major temples to be constructed before the advent of Islam.

The rites and prescriptions of Islam required different architectural forms, and the anthropomorphism of Hindu–Buddhism was taboo. The earlier structures were simply abandoned, if they were not pulled apart for their masonry, as happened to Kraton Ratu Boko. But the strength of the past, and the Javanese ability to assimilate, meant that they were not destroyed. Even now, fresh offerings can be found every day in front of the statues of Siva and his wife Durga at Prambanan.

The temples then suffered more by neglect and nature, the frequent earthquakes and heavy rain of the region contributing to their decay.

The Dutch established themselves on the north coast of Central Java at Semarang in 1678, leaving the rump of the Mataram kingdoms to the south to their own devices to a certain degree, though with the benefit of a Dutch advisory 'resident'. The VOC officials were interested in cash flows rather than culture; they did not even notice Prambanan when they passed by it on the road from Surakarta to Yogyakarta. But in 1778, Radermacher, the founder of the first masonic lodge in Batavia, established the 'Batavian Society for the Arts and Sciences', under the influence of the Enlightenment. It was the first scholarly organization of its kind in the East. The transactions of this society were maintained to the end of the nineteenth century.

After a brief Napoleonic interlude, the British took over the administration of Java. In 1811, Thomas Stamford Raffles was created Lieutenant-Governor of Java by the Governor-General of India. It was Raffles who was the first to understand the importance of Borobudur. In 1814, he ordered Cornelius, a surveyor at Semarang, to inspect the monument. After visiting Borobudur on 18 May 1815, Raffles noted in his Journal:

> In addition to their claim on the consideration of the antiquarian, the ruins of two of these places, Brambana and Boro Bodo, are admirable as majestic works of art, the great extent of the masses of buildings covered, in some parts, with the luxuriant vegetation of the climate, the beauty and delicate execution of the separate portions, the symmetry and regularity of the whole, the great number and interesting character of the statues and the bas-reliefs, with which they are ornamented, excite our wonder that they were not earlier examined, sketched and described.

Raffles, following the example of Marsden's *The History of Sumatra* (1811), wrote *The History of Java* which appeared in London in 1817. This quite remarkable book, however, only mentions the antiquities briefly. But Borobudur is described in it for the first time and all the monuments are grouped as being of the same period, with Candi Sukuh on Mount Lawu correctly being considered as of a different period. Raffles's main collaborator, John Crawfurd, published in 1820 in Edinburgh his *History of the Indian Archipelago*. This book was taken up and enlarged in 1856 with the title of *A Descriptive Dictionary of the Indian Islands and Adjacent Countries*. Crawfurd was enthusiastic about the architecture he described, but disapproved of the sculpture. After this activity stimulated by Raffles, several years passed without anything new being written about the monumental art of Java.

However, knowledge about the Javanese monuments began to spread. The philosopher, Amiel, made allusion to them in his *Journal* in 1866, and finally the Batavian Society published the work of Leemans, who made much use of the drawings of Cornelius, supplemented with others by J. Wilsen and Schönberg Mulder. The book appeared in 1873 in Dutch and in French. At more or less the same time, in 1872, the Batavian Society commissioned a complete photographic survey of the monument. The photographer appointed, Kinsbergen, gave up the idea of covering it completely. He found that the monument was not completely cleared and complained that there were four feet of debris in some parts. For the first time in reports, mention is made of the subsidence of the first and third galleries. Kinsbergen, when he cleared the paving, also undertook the first restoration work. He filled the hollows in the paving with sand so that the rainwater would run out of the gargoyles, instead of staying in the gallery. Two of the prints of these first photographs were found by Ségalen among the papers of Gauguin in Tahiti, and one of them, showing a relief on the first gallery, is probably the inspiration for the painting called 'Et l'or de leur corps' which can be seen in the Musée d'Orsay.

The work of clearing the monument continued. This led to the discovery of the hidden reliefs by the Dutch archaeologist Brandes in 1886. These were excavated under the direction of Ijzerman in 1890. After these discoveries, interest in the monument grew and the decision to restore Borobudur was made. The work was carried out from 1907 to 1911 under Van Erp. The means at his disposal were very limited so he could not undertake even a partial dismantling of the monument. He tried to stabilize the walls by getting rid of the rainwater permeating the foundations. He used the same method for this as Kinsbergen, but instead of filling the hollows with sand he used concrete of very varied quality. This was covered over with a paving of andesite which allowed the water to flow out of the original gargoyles. When concrete was not necessary, the joints in the original paving were opened and filled with mortar.

The circular terraces were entirely relaid with new material on the ruins of the old and the pierced stupas were completely reconstructed, some with new stones. After this work, Borobudur regained something of its original appearance. It was not until 1931 that a law was enacted protecting historic monuments in Indonesia. Archaeological research continued and mention is made in this text of some of the more important contributions.

Van Erp's restoration work was shown to be insufficient. The monument continued to shift and different parts were dismantled to avoid collapse, especially the balustrades on the north side. Soekmono launched in 1968 the 'Save Borobudur' appeal which was taken up by the Indonesian government and UNESCO. They ordered numerous studies of the climatic conditions, local earthquakes, the settlement which had occurred since 1914, the structure of the surrounding soils, local petrography, biology, and botany in relation to the monument. The conclusion of these studies was that the damage caused to Borobudur came essentially from the rainwater and the existence of a large amount of water in the hill which escapes through the joints in the vertical stone walls and leaves particles of soil on the surface of the reliefs. The humidity leads to a growth of algae, mosses, lichens, fungi, and bacteria. The general recommendations behind the project were, first, to eliminate the water coming from the hill by installing a suitable drainage system, secondly, to clean the bas-reliefs and remove all the growths on the surface of the stone and, thirdly, to re-erect the monument.

The project was prepared on the civil engineering side by a Dutch firm, and United Nations experts and personnel supplied by several countries under bilateral aid programmes to Indonesia advised on the treatment of the stone and the problems involved in the restoration. The project was divided into three main phases: dismantling, treatment of the stone, and reconstruction. It was considered that the upper terraces which had been restored by Van Erp were in sufficiently good condition and did not have to be dismantled. The base, being well preserved, was in no need of restoration either. The work was therefore limited to the galleries containing the bas-reliefs. The dismantling by itself was relatively simple, but given the large number of stones—more than 1,600,000—the numbering had to be done very carefully and under close supervision. The difficulty of finding a wrongly numbered stone can easily be imagined.

As mentioned earlier, the monument is mainly constructed with andesite, a stone of volcanic origin. However, it is not the classic type and is closer to augite andesite which can be found all around the Pacific. This stone has a porosity that varies greatly from 11 to 46 per cent. The highly porous nature of the stone encourages vegetal growths. The mosses are very difficult to eliminate, since the atmospheric humidity is sufficient to sustain their growth. The ferns can survive on very little earth but can probably be entirely eliminated. The lichens form by far the most widespread growths and are difficult to destroy because, like the mosses, they can live off the humidity in the atmosphere. They cause the greatest damage to the structure, apart from the unlovely appearance they give to the stone. Some lichens are acidic and in contact with rainwater can cause the stones underneath them to be eroded. The roots of the lichens also penetrate the pores of the stone and cause them to split. Finally, the algae are often found together with the mosses, and in these cases hasten the corrosion of the stone. They develop, above all, in the water coming from the hill underneath the monument.

Depending on whether a stone is merely exposed to rainwater or additionally to water coming from the hill, it can be the host to different growths and consequently suffer different kinds of damage. This can be seen in the monument where the changes in the balustrades are not the same as those in the retaining walls which are in contact with the hill. It was decided, therefore, to eliminate as much as possible, if not all, the water seeping out of the hill. To do this, the restoration project involved the provision of two successive shields of araldite, a tar epoxy adhesive (Figure 9). Water was to be

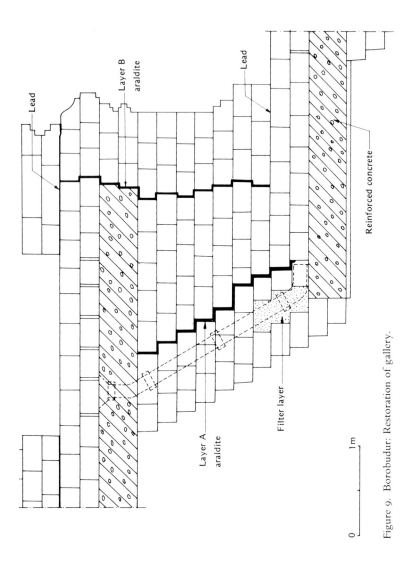

Figure 9. Borobudur: Restoration of gallery.

Lead

Layer B araldite

Lead

Reinforced concrete

Layer A araldite

Filter layer

0   1 m

retained behind the walls, collected on concrete slabs, and led away by a drainage system to the edges of the hill. The stones broken by the lichens had to be put together again. It is possible that the protective shields will not eliminate the growths for which the atmospheric humidity is sufficient to survive. Consequently, some of the lichens and mosses will reappear especially where the stone has itself as high a porosity as 46 per cent.

The main interest of the project was not in the treatment of the stone but in the mechanical aspects of the dismantling of the monument and the means used to reconstruct it. Borobudur (as was seen in Chapter 4) is constructed on a natural hill, enlarged by fill which supports the stone structure. The abundant rainfall of Central Java (about 2 074 mm a year) gets through to the fill and carries away fine particles as it seeps out. This causes the noticeable shifting of the monument which can be as much as 10°. The extraordinary cohesion of the masonry has stood up to these movements but the settlement of the monument has been considerable, by as much as 80 cm.

Van Erp did not try to correct these effects, particularly on the circular terraces, the ruins of which were disguised by rebuilding with new stones, sometimes very freely. As, moreover, the base has not been touched, the calculation of the new measurements had to be made within these limits, that is, between the base and the first circular terrace; this is in spite of re-erecting the walls of the balustrades and the bas-reliefs. Several adjustments to the levels were therefore necessary so that the first circular terrace was not obliterated.

The re-erection of the structure was carried out on reinforced concrete slabs about 5 m wide which completely surround the monument at 45 cm below the level of the reconstructed paving and under each of the galleries and balustrade walls. These four cement rings have given a new cohesion to the monument, for the settlement and the dismantling have reduced the holding quality of the original structure. This explains the need for considerable stability in the concrete slabs which are 60 cm thick and which have to stand up to seismic jolts as well as the normal stresses and strains caused by the building. Borobudur is located in a zone where there is a fair amount of earthquake activity.

To prevent continual removal from the fill by the permeating water causing a constant sinking, a layer of sand, the grain size of which decreases from the top to the bottom, was laid to hold back the earth from the fill while still allowing the water to flow away.

In sum, the internal stability of the monument now rests on five slabs of reinforced concrete corresponding to each of the galleries and the upper level supporting the circular terraces. On these slabs the walls containing the bas-reliefs and the balustrades have been reconstructed. Internally, they are protected by two screens of araldite and at the base by a lead sheet to prevent upward capillary action. This is completed by a filter which keeps back the particles of the fill and stops them being carried off by the water permeating through the monument. All this work, even though aided by modern equipment, took several years to complete, for the size of the restoration operation, substantially completed by 1984, was considerable.

7

Conclusion

THE architecture of Indian origin in Java is closely linked to its religious meaning. The techniques used are not designed to improve on architectural volume but, on the contrary, the designers readily acknowledge the laws of gravity. All the same, it is not true that purely architectural considerations were absent from Borobudur and the monuments nearby. This can most easily be seen in the proportion and outline of the cornice. For example, the mouldings on the hidden foot at Borobudur are very powerful. The architect knew how to capture the light on the broad concave and convex line of the moulding which is emphasized by the dark area under the semicircular projecting edge. Beneath this there is deep shadow at any hour of the day because the projection is sufficiently broad. The shadows on the curves of the moulding, however, change according to the time of day and give variety to the surface.

The horizontality of Borobudur has often been remarked upon and is not the work of an insensitive designer. What is perhaps remarkable is that, after all its numerous alterations, the monument manages to preserve an idea of unity. This was deliberately sought at the end of the second and third periods of construction when the architect was able to give the impression of there being a single concept behind the building by adding decoration to the cornices and new doorways to the lower galleries.

The architectural forms created at Borobudur did not have time to have much influence since the Hindu expansion came too quickly after the monument was completed. Even if, historically, the reigning princes made an effort not to antagonize the Buddhist community, the Buddhist movement was spent. Plaosan is the last of the great Buddhist buildings in Java.

If the horizontal lines are dominant in Borobudur, Candi Sari, and Plaosan, it is the vertical lines which become of major importance in Prambanan. There the attention is directed to the summit and, perhaps more than at Borobudur, it can be seen what little importance is attached to architectural volume in the way the monument is conceived. With Prambanan it is really a case of reconstructing a mountain. There is no relationship between the size of the cellas and the amount of masonry used in the building. To enhance the apparent height of the building, tricks in perspective were introduced, by reducing the distance between the horizontal bands as one gets nearer the top and accentuating the natural perspective. The moulding has, however, lost much of its importance and strength. The wealth of decoration gives a kind of resonance to the outline, so much so that the upper parts are difficult to distinguish clearly. Though Borobudur had little architectural influence, Prambanan was the model for many temples of the thirteenth and fourteenth centuries in east Java.

The symbolic significance of the monument has profoundly evolved. Borobudur, in its first state, was not a mandala, a figure, an instrument aiding meditation. It became this in its second state, but accidents which occurred during the construction gradually caused the original meaning of the monument to be forgotten, though for the first Buddhist devotees the monument was without ambiguity. It is likely that ritual played a large part in the architectural composition. The believer, passing through the galleries, in some way relived the life of the Buddhas and the Bodhisattvas.

This first meaning became overloaded with the passage of time with theories wilfully complicating the significance of the structure. When European scholars tried to unravel the meaning of Borobudur they faced an impossible task, and the monument has become a real apple of discord among different schools of thought. The Western visitor, for his part, has his own cultural baggage and makes his own cultural references.

Sometimes the sculptor himself has changed the meaning of the image he is illustrating. For instance, in the first gallery to the west, a relief shows three palaces which the father of the future Buddha gave to his son, but as the relief comes after that showing his marriage, the sculptor allowed himself the licence of showing a love scene in three episodes. Bedtime is illustrated in the first palace, the second palace entirely closed, and in the third the prince watches his wife dressing. The real subject of the relief—the gift of the palaces—is overlooked, and the interest the panels have for the visitor is quite different from the original intention of the scene.

Since the sixteenth century, Islam became firmly established in Java but the taste for syncretism remains very strong among the Javanese. When Borobudur became accessible once more, it naturally assumed the significance of a holy place where contact with the spirits was possible.

Glossary

Avolekitisvara. An important Bodhisattva of compassion in Mahayana Buddhism.

Bodhisattva. A future Buddha, one who is able to reach Nirvana but delays doing so through compassion of suffering beings (in Sanskrit 'one whose essence is perfect knowledge').

Buddha. A historical person, Siddartha Gautama, *c.*563–483 BC who preached a doctrine of renunciation.

Candi. A general Indonesian term for an ancient temple or shrine.

Dieng. A high volcanic plateau containing the earliest (Hindu) monuments in central Java.

Hinayana Buddhism. The Buddhism of the Lesser Vehicle, so called scornfully by Mahayanists, and which adheres strictly to early Buddhist traditions.

Jina. (The Dhyani Buddhas), the transcendental Buddhas of meditation: Vairocana, the illuminated one, Aksobhya, the imperturbable one, Ratnasambhava, issued from a jewel, Amithaba, infinite light, and Amoghasida, eternal success.

Mahayana Buddhism. Buddhism of the Greater Vehicle; Mahayanism through magic, rituals, formulae, gymnastics, and breath control shortens the number of rebirths before reaching Nirvana.

Maitreya. The next Buddha.

Makara. A mythical beast used as an architectural decoration, especially at the end of string-walls on stairways.

Mandala. A symbolic geometrical figure, often circular, representing the Universe (from the Sanskrit meaning 'disc').

Manjusri. A distant future Buddha, of importance in Mahayana Buddhism.

Mount Meru. The cosmic mountain, the home of the pantheon of Hindu gods and axis of the world, around which oceans and continents are arranged.

Nirvana. A state of perfect bliss and release from karma, attained by the extinction of individuality (often popularly but incorrectly equated with heaven).

Prajnaparamita. A goddess in Mahayana Buddhism.

Sailendra. A Buddhist Javanese dynasty of the eighth–ninth centuries.

Sanjaya. A Hindu-Javanese dynasty of the eighth–ninth centuries which at first appears to have shared power with the Sailendras but was dominant from 832.

Sanskrit. The ancient and sacred language of the Hindus in India, not used as a vernacular for around 2,000 years.

Stele (also 'stela'). An upright slab or pillar usually with an inscription and carving.

Tang. A Chinese dynasty ruling from 618–*c.*906.

Tantra. An esoteric variant of Buddhism much influenced by the mystical and magical.

Tara. Goddess of importance in Tantric Buddhism.

VOC. Verenidge Oostindische Compagnie, the Dutch East India Company, 1602–1799.

Select Bibliography

Abbreviations

BEFEO Bulletin de l'Ecole Française d'Extrême Orient
TBG Tijdschrift voor Indische Taal-, Land- en Volkenkunde uitgeg-
even door het (Koninklijke) Bataviaasch Genootschap van Kunsten en
Wetenschappen

* * * *

Battacharya, K., *L'Atman Brahman dans le boudhisme ancien*, Paris, 1973.
Bernet-Kempers, A. J., *Ancient Indonesian Art*, Amsterdam, 1959.
————, *Herstel in eigen waarde monumentzorg in Indonesia*, Den Haag,
1978.
Bosch, F. D. K., 'A hypothesis as to the origin of Hindu Javanese Art',
Rupam, No. 17, Janvier, 1924.
————, 'De inscriptie von Kelorak', *TBG*, LXVIII, 1928.
————, *Selected studies in Indonesian archaeology*, The Hague, 1961.
Buchari, 'Preliminary report of an Old Malay inscription at Sodjo-
merto', 1966 (unpublished note).
de Casparis, J. G., *Inscripties uit de Çailendra tijd* (Prasasti Indonesia I),
Bandung, 1950.
————, *Selected inscriptions from the 7th to the 9th century A.D.* (Prasasti
Indonesia II), Bandung, 1956.
————, 'New evidence on cultural relations between Java and Ceylon
in ancient times', *Artibus Asiae*, XXIV, 1961.
Coedès, G., 'Les inscriptions de Bat Cum', *Journal Asiatique*, CXC,
1908.
————, *Pour mieux comprendre Angkor*, Paris, 1947 (English translation
Angkor, Kuala Lumpur, 1963).
————, *Les états hindouisés d'Indochine et d'Indonésie*, Paris, 1968.
Conze, E., *Le Bouddhisme dans son essence et son developpement*, Paris,
1951
Coomaraswamy, A. K., *History of India and Indonesian Art*, 1927.
Damais, L. C., 'Etudes d'Epigraphie indonésienne', *BEFEO*, XLV,
1951, *BEFEO*, XLVI, 1952, *BEFEO*, LVI, 1968.

Dumarçay, J., *Candi Sewu et l'architecture bouddhique du centre de Java*, Paris, 1982.

———, *The Temples of Java*, Singapore, 1986.

Dupont, P., 'Les Buddhas dits d'Amaravati en Asie du Sud-Est', *BEFEO*, XLIX, 1958.

Foucher, A., 'Notes d'Archéologie bouddhique', *BEFEO*, IX, 1909.

Groslier, B. P., *Inscriptions du Bayon*, Paris, 1973.

Hoenig, A., *Das Formproblem des Borobudur*, 1924.

Ijzerman, J. W., *Beschrijving der Oudheden nabij de grens der residentie's Soerakarta en Djogdjakarta*, about 1880.

Krom, N. J., *Archeological Description of Barabudur*, The Hague, 1927.

Lamotte, E., *Histoire du Bouddhisme indien des origines à l'ère Saka*, Louvain, 1958.

Le Bonheur, A., *La sculpture indonésienne au Musée Guimet*, Paris, 1971.

Leemans, C., *Boro-budur dans l'île de Java*, Leide, 1874.

Macdonald, W., 'Review of Van Erp *Beschrijving van Barabudur*, *TBG*, LXXII, 1932.

Moens, J. L., '*Barabudur, Mendut en Pawon un hum onderlinge samenhang*', *TBG*, LXXXIV, 1951.

Mus, P., 'Barabudur, esquisse d'une histoire du bouddhisme fondée sur la critique archéologique des textes', *BEFEO*, XXXII, XXXIII, XXXIV, 1933–5.

Parmentier, H., 'L'architecture interpretée dans les bas-reliefs anciens de Java', *BEFEO*, VII, 1907.

Pelliot, Paul, 'Deux itinéraires de Chine en Inde', *BEFEO*, IV, 1905.

Permatilleke, L. and Silva, R., 'A Buddhist monastery type of ancient Ceylon showing Mahayanist influence', *Artibus Asiae*, XXX/1, 1968.

Pigeaud, Th., *Java in the 14th century, I-V*, The Hague, 1960–3.

Pott, P. H., *Yoga and Yantra*, The Hague, 1966.

Raffles, T. S., *History of Java*, London, 1817.

Smithies, M., *Yogyakarta: Cultural Heart of Indonesia*, Singapore, 1986.

Soekmono, 'The archaeology of Central Java before 800 A.D.' (stencilled pamphlet), London, 1973.

———, *Candi, fungsi dan pengertiannya*, Jakarta, 1974.

Stohr, W. and Zoetmulder, P., *Les religions d'Indonésie*, Paris, 1968.

Stutterheim, T., *Tjandi Baraboedur, Naam, Virm en Beteekenis*, Batavia, 1929 (English translation: *Studies in Indonesian archeology*, The Hague, 1956).

Van Erp, T., *Barabudur, architectural description*, The Hague, 1931.

Van Leur, J. C., *Indonesian trade and society*, The Hague, 1955.

Van Lohuizen de Leew, J. E., 'South East Asian architecture and the stupa of Nandangarh', *Artibus Asiae*, XIX, 1956.

de Vink, J., *Report on an excavation on the east side of the Borobudur*, Leyden, 1912.

Vlekke, B. H. M., *Nusantara, A history of Indonesia*, The Hague, 1960.

Zimmer, H., *Kunstform und yoga in indischen Kultbild*, Berlin, 1926.

Chronological Table

DATES A.D.	KINGS — SANJAYA	KINGS — SAILENDRA	BOROBUDUR	BUILDINGS	EVENTS
?	Sanjaya				
732				The Cangal Inscription	
752 ?		Bhanu			
?		Visnu			Sailendra raids in Indo-China
760 ?	Panongkaran			Mendut I?	
775			Construction begun		
778				Kalasan I	
780 ?	Panunggalan			Sewu I	
782		Indra	Borobudur I	Kalasan II	
792			Borobudur II	Sewu II	
800 ?	Warak		Borobudur III	Kalasan III, Mendut II	
802				Sari	The Khmer king, Jayavarman II, frees himself from Javanese suzerainty
819	Garung	Samaratunga	Borobudur IV	Plaosan I	
824				Beginning of construction of Prambanan	Appearance of the double wall-facing technique
832				Mendut III	
				Plaosan II	
			Borobudur V	Prambanan II	
				Asu	
842	Pikatan				
856	Kayuwani				

Index

Abhayagiri Vihara, 11
Agastya, 3
Aksobhya, 9, 54
Amaravati, 8, 10
Amiel, Henri Frédéric, 59
Amithaba, 9, 54
Amoghasida, 9, 54
Ananda, 9
Andesite, 22, 29, 53, 59, 61
Angkor, 22
Angkor Wat, 40
Anthropomorphism, 57
Anuradhapura, 11
Architectural illustrations, 15–18
Arjuna, 14
Artisans, 2
Asceticism, 6
Ashlar, 31
Avalokitesvara, 44
Awada, 41

Bali, 57
Batavian Society for the Arts and
    Sciences, 58–9
Bayon, 31, 55
Benares, 7, 41, 43–4
Bernier, François, 45
Bhadratjari, 42
Bhanu, King, 2
Bima, 14
Bodh Gaya, 6
Bodhisattvas, 6, 8–9, 41–2, 44, 51–4
Borobudur: and Manasara, 18; and
    Raffles, 58; approach to, 30; arches,
    24, 29; architecture, 30–44, 65–7;
    balustrades, 25, 28, 40–3; Buddhas,
    25, 41–3; central structure, 24–5;

chronology, 5; construction
    periods, 22–8; construction
    techniques, 28–30; decline of, 28;
    duality of, 4, 21; entrance
    doorways, 24, 28; façade, 34; foot,
    23–5, 31, 39–40, 65; foundation,
    22–3; galleries, 23–5, 28, 30–2,
    35–8, 40–2, 61, 67; gargoyles, 39,
    59; gateways, 40; gutters, 25, 39;
    horizontally, 65–6; monastery, 32;
    pinnacles, 42; plan, 17, 26–7;
    platform, 43; reliefs, 24, 28–30, 32,
    34–8, 40–2, 64, 67; restoration of,
    59–64; scaffolding, 23; site, 21–2;
    stairways, 23–5, 28–32, 39; string-
    walls, 25, 33; stucco, 29–30; stupas,
    25, 42–4, 60; subsidence, 24, 28;
    terraces, 25, 30–2, 43, 60;
    walkways, 23
Bosch, F. D. K., 47, 54
Brahma, 7
Brahmins, 7
Brandes, Jan Laurens Andries, 59
British, 58
Bronze drums, 16
Buddha, 6–8, 40–1, 44–5, 54, 67;
    statues, 10–11, 14, 25, 41–3, 49
Buddhism, 6; and Borobudur, 4, 6,
    21, 66; and Hinduism, 6; in
    Indonesia, 10–11, 47; see also
    Hinayana Buddhism; Mahayana
    Buddhism; Tantric Buddhism;
    Vajrayana school of Buddhism
Buddhist: architecture, 47–56;
    doctrine, 7–10; monasteries, 10;
    monks, 10; monuments, 14, 54–5,
    65; mythology, 1; saints, 10;

sanctuaries, 3, 10, 14; temples, 13–14, 18; texts, 39–42
Budur, 5
Building techniques, 15–16, 19–20, 29

Cambodia, 3; building techniques, 20, 29
Canal, 2
Candi Arjuna, 18
Candi Brahma, 56
Candi Bubrah, 51
Candi Cangal, 5, 13, 15
Candi Ceto, 57
Candi Kalasan, 4, 13, 20, 29, 47–9, 53
Candi Lumbung, 14, 51
Candi Mendut, 21, 30, 44–5
Candi Muncul, 15
Candi Pawon, 30, 44–5
Candi Plaosan, 10, 47, 51, 53–4, 65–6
Candi Prambanan, 3, 5, 40, 47, 53, 55–7, 66
Candi Sambisari, 15, 56–7
Candi Sari, 47, 51–4, 66
Candi Sewu, 4–5, 14, 20, 47, 49–51, 54
Candi Siva, 56
Candi Sukuh, 57–8
Candi Visnu, 56
Cangal inscription, 2, 13
de Casparis, J. G., 2–3, 11, 44, 53, 55
Ceylon, 11
Chinese: building techniques, 15–16, 19; chronicles, 1, 3; emperor, 3
Coedès, G., 3
Conze, E., 8
Cornelius, B., 58–9
Crawfurd, John, 58

Descriptive Dictionary of the Indian Islands and Adjacent Countries, 58
Dharmatunga, King, see Visnu
Dhyani Buddhas, see Jinas, the five
Dieng, 4; temples, 3, 5, 14–15, 18

Dong-Son civilization, 16
Durga, 57
Dutch, 57
Dyana, 7

Ecstasies, see Dyana
Elo River, 21, 30

Foucher, A., 7

Gandawyuha, 42
Ganges River, 7, 22
Garung (Patapan?), King, 2
Gatotkaca, 14
Gauguin, 59
Gazelles, 44
Gedong Songo, 15
Gnomon, 19
Gunung Wukir, 4–5, 13

Hartman (Resident of Kedu), 43
Himalayas, 6
Hinayana Buddhism, 8–9, 11
Hindu: buildings, 4, 18; monuments, 13–15; mythology, 1; period, 1–2; priests, 1; renaissance, 3, 55; sanctuaries, 14; temples, 18, 55
Hinduism: and Borobudur, 4, 21; in Indonesia, 18, 57
History of Java, 58
History of Sumatra, 58
History of the Indian Archipelago, 58
Houi Ning, 11

Ijzerman, J. W., 59
India, 1, 3, 8, 14, 20
Indian priests, 15, 18
Indo-China, 3
Indonesian government, 60
Indra (Sangramadhanomjaya), King, 2–3, 44
Inscriptions, see Stele
Islam, 57, 67

Jakarta, 2
Jatakamala, 41
Java, 3–4; embassies from China, 3;
    reuniting of central and east, 3, 5
Javanese, 3; Buddhists, 10
Jayavarman II, 3
Jayavarman VII, 55
Jember, 11
Jinas, the five, 4, 6, 9, 54
Jumna River, 22

Kalasan inscription, 2, 21
Kapilavastu, 6–7
Karmawibhangga, 39
Kayuwani, King, 2
Kediri, 57
Kedu, 43
Kelurak, 14
Khmer monuments, 30–1; prince, 53
Kinsbergen, Isidore van, 59
Kraton Ratu Boko, 11, 56–7
Kusinagara, 8

La Fontaine, Jean de, 45
Lalitavistara, 40, 42
Leemans, C., 59
Linga, 13, 18–19, 56
Lions, 16, 20, 39
Lumbini, 6, 32, 40

Magada, 8
Magelang, 22
Mahasanghika, 8
Mahayana Buddhism, 1, 3, 6, 8–9, 11,
    44, 47, 54
Majapahit, 57
Makara, 39
Malang, 3
Manasara, 18–19
Mandala, 14, 47, 49, 54–5, 66
Manjusri, 14, 44, 54
Mara, 41
Marsden, William, 58
Mataram, 2; kingdoms, 57

Maya, Queen, 32, 40
Mayamata, 18–19
Monuments, 13–15
Mount Lawu, 57–8
Mount Meru, 56–7

Neak Phean, 22
Negarakertagama, 5
New History of the Tang, 3
Nganjuk, 54
Nirvana, 8–9

Old Javanese: inscription, 39; text, 6

Pala dynasty, 11
Pallava dynasty, 14, 16, 20
Pancatantra, 45
Panongkaran, King, 2
Panunggalan, King, 2
Patapan, King, *see* Garung
Pelliot, Paul, 3
Penataran, 57
Pikatan, Rakai, 2, 53–5
Potteries: Tang period, 5
Pradakshina, 10
Prajnaparamita, 8
Prajnaparamita, 10
Prambanan, 11, 14; temple, *see* Candi
    Prambanan
Princes, 2
Progo River, 4, 21, 30
Puntadewa, 14
Purnavarman, King, 2

Radermacher, Jacob Cornelius
    Matthew, 57
Raffles, Thomas Stamford, 58
Ramayana, 56
Ratnasambhava, 9, 54
Rebirth, *see* Samsara

Sailendra dynasty, 2–4, 55
Sakya clan, 6
Sakyamuni, *see* Buddha

Samantabhadra, 42, 44
Samaratunga, King, 2–3
Sambisari, 15
Samsara, 7, 9.
Sang Hyang Kamahayanikan, 6, 47
Sangramadhanomjaya, King, *see* Indra
Sanjaya: dynasty, 2–5, 54; King, 2, 13
Sanskrit, 1; architectural treatises,
    18–20; inscriptions, 1–3, 6, 13–14;
    texts, 11
'Save Borobudur' appeal, 60
Schonberg Mulder, 59
Ségalen, Victor, 59
Semar, 14
Semarang, 57
Sembodro, 14
Sempaga, 10
Siddartha Gautama, *see* Buddha
Singosari, 57
Sinhalese: building techniques, 20, 29;
    chronicles, 11
Siva, 56–7
Soekmono, 60
Solo, 57
Srikandi, 14
Statues, 10–11, 14, 25, 41–5, 49, 51,
    53–4
Stele, 13–14, 21
Stone architecture, 15–16
Stupas, 8, 10, 16–18, 21, 25, 42–4, 53
Sudhana, 42
Sulawesi, 16
Sumatra, 16

Ta Kev, 31
Tang dynasty, 5, 19
Tantra, 9
Tantric Buddhism, 9–10, 54
Tara, goddess, 6, 10, 13, 21, 51, 54
Taruma, 2
Temples of Java, 55
Tidar, 22

UNESCO, 60
Ungaran, 15
University of Nalanda, 11

Vairocana, 9, 54
Vajradhara Buddhist sect, 5
Vajradhatu mandala, 14, 54
Vajrayana school of Buddhism, 9
Van Erp, T., 59–60, 63
Vijayarama stupa, 11
Visnu (Dharmatunga?), King, 2
Visvakarman, 16–18
VOC, 57
Void, 8–9
Volcanic tuff, 22, 53

Warak, King, 2
Wheel of the Law, 43–4
Wilsen, J., 59
Wooden architecture, 15–16, 19
Wringin Putih, 30

Yoga, 6